MODERN BRITAIN

An Introduction

*For Christina and Tom
with love*

MODERN BRITAIN

An Introduction

John L. Irwin

ROUTLEDGE

First published 1976
by Unwin Hyman Ltd
Second edition 1987
Third impression 1990

Reprinted 1993
by Routledge
11 New Fetter Lane, London EC4P 4EE

Printed in Great Britain by Biddles Ltd,
Guildford and King's Lynn

British Library Cataloguing in Publication Data

A catalogue record for this book is available from the British Library

ISBN 0–415–09902–1 (pbk)

Contents

Preface
to the First Edition

In writing a book like this, one of the most difficult tasks is to decide what should be put in and what should be left out. It is obviously impossible to give a fully comnprehensive account of all aspects of every British institution in a book of this length, but nevertheless I hope that it will at least serve as an introduction to some of the key features of modern British life. Another problem is that Britain is not a static society. During the writing of the book many things have changed, while others are still in the course of changing. Whenever possible account has been taken of new developments and I hope that the reader is not too irritated if he finds that an institution described in the book has changed its function, been modified or, possibly, disappeared altogether. Perhaps it may serve to prove that Britain is not quite as conservative as he thought; some things do change!

I must acknowledge the assistance of many people in writing this book, a large number of them being my former students at the University of Turku and the Turku School of Economics. It was their questions and (frequently critical) comments about British institutions that first persuaded me that it should be written. I should also thank my former colleagues at both these institutions for their help and advice, in particular George Maude and Geoffrey Alcock, both of whom were good enough to read the manuscript and make helpful suggestions. Of course none of those who have assisted me bear any responsibility for what I have written – that is mine alone.

My greatest debt is to my wife, Merga, for the help, encouragement and patience, while I should also acknowledge the tolerance of my children, who (most of the time) allowed me to work in peace.

Preface
to the Second Edition

Since the first edition of this book appeared in 1976 there have been a number of radical changes in British society. The Conservative Government that came to power in 1979 has pursued policies that have been further to the right than those of any other administration since the Second World War and this has had far reaching effects on many aspects of British life. At the same time Britain, like many other countries, has experienced economic difficulties during the last decade as a result of the adverse trading conditions that have existed following the increase in oil prices in the early 1970s. In the second edition of *Modern Britain* I have retained the basic format of the first edition, but have tried to update the text and bring in new information whenever appropriate. I have also added a chapter on Northern Ireland which attempts to place events in the province in perspective.

As with the first edition I have had assistance from a number of people and I would like to thank in particular Sheila McLean, Bruce Kendall, Sally Green and Peter Allen, all of whom have been generous enough to help me with the preparation of the second edition. As with the first edition all errors and interpretations are of course my own. I must also thank my wife, Merja, who prepared the index.

1

Introduction to Britain

The British Isles are situated off the north-west coast of Europe. At one time they were part of the European landmass, but following the last great ice age the level of the sea rose, and the land area which now forms the British Isles became separated from the rest of the Continent by a stretch of water. It is true that at its narrowest point this water is only some twenty miles wide, but those twenty miles have had a great effect on the development of Britain, for the gap is not only physical, it is psychological too. Britain is at the same time part of, but separate from, Europe, and this has had far-reaching implications for the development of all aspects of life – social, political, economic and linguistic.

The fact that Britain is on the western side of the European continent meant that when trade routes went overland to the East, Britain was on the fringe of Europe, and was virtually ignored. With the discovery of the New World in the late fifteenth and early sixteenth centuries, and the development of ocean trade routes, Britain became more important. She was in a position to dominate western trade and was not slow to take advantage of this. As Britain was an island she had to depend on shipping for her contact with her neighbours, whether she wanted to trade with them or fight them. This meant that the British had to be conversant with ships and the sea. The new trade routes lay across the oceans and Britain was to build the basis of her power and wealth on her navies.

Island states have usually found that the sea can be both an advantage and a disadvantage as far as defence is concerned. Although the sea can provide a moat, it can also be a highway for invaders, and this has been so in the case of Britain. Until 1066 the North Sea and the English Channel were a wide highway, on which invaders from

Germany, Scandinavia and Normandy sailed at different times. After 1066, however, the seas proved to be a moat; for since that date there has been no successful military invasion of Britain by a foreign power. This is very important for an understanding of British institutions, for it has meant that following the Norman Conquest, with its far-reaching implications for English society, foreign institutions and customs have never been forcibly imposed on the British. Thus the form of government, the legal system and many other aspects of British life have developed in a particularly British, some would say insular, way. This is not to say, of course, that Britain has been completly free of foreign influence throughout her history. However ideas, institutions and other contributions from overseas have not been introduced by an invading army or occupying force, nor have foreign customs and ways of life been forced upon the inhabitants against their will.

This freedom from invasion can be attributed to a number of factors, one of the most important being the English Channel itself. Although wider seas than the Channel have been successfully crossed – while the British themselves have on more than one occasion invaded Europe across the Channel – the fact remains that whenever invasion has threatened, the British have managed to retain control of the waters between Britain and the Continent. Another factor that should be taken into consideration is that Britain is not on the way to anywhere. It is true that Britain lies on the sea routes to the Americas, but by definition a sea route does not go overland. Continental industrialists and merchants wanting to develop their trade with the New World could easily avoid Britain by sailing round her coasts. Nor do any other countries lie on the far side of Britain, so she has never been used as a corridor through which foreign armies have marched or fought, as has been the fate of countries such as Belgium, Finland and Poland. Should, however, a situation develop in the future in which the United States, or any other American country, wanted to attack Europe, it is probable that Britain would be the first country to fall. The attacker could then use British territory as a base for subsequent operations. Indeed this has already happened, with the compliance and assistance of the British Government and people. In 1944 Europe was invaded by a force that had a very large North American contingent, and an American commander.

It has already been mentioned that the British Isles lie off the north-west coast of Europe. To be more precise, the 0° meridian passes through Greenwich (slightly east of London), while latitude

50°N passes through the Lizard peninsula, in the south of England, and latitude 60°N lies across the Shetlands, off the north coast of Scotland. From the south coast to the northern-most point on the Scottish mainland is a distance of just under 600 miles (966 kilometres), while the east and west coasts are about 300 miles (483 kilometres) apart at their widest point.

Geographically, the British Isles are made up of a number of islands, and there are also a number of different political components. Very often 'England' is used as a synonym for Britain, while 'Englishman' is employed as a blanket description for all the inhabitants of the British Isles. This, as any Welshman, Irishman, or Scot will quickly point out, is incorrect. The United Kingdom consists of England and Wales, Scotland and Northern Ireland. The Isle of Man, in the Irish Sea, and the Channel Islands, off the coast of France (and formerly part of the Duchy of Normandy), are not part of the United Kingdom. They are Crown dependencies, with their own legislative assemblies and legal systems. The Irish Republic, Southern Ireland, is politically entirely separate from the United Kingdom, and has been so since 1922. The term Great Britain is used to describe the three countries of England, Wales and Scotland. The total land area of the United Kingdom is 93,025 square miles (240,934 sq km), made up as follows: England, 50,052 (129,634); Wales, 7,968 (20,637); Scotland, 29,799 (77,179); and Northern Ireland 5,206 (13,484). The Isle of Man has an area of 227 square miles (588 sq km) and the Channel Islands, 75 square miles (194 sq km).

England became a united kingdom in the ninth century and Wales, which had formerly been a principality, was incorporated into this kingdom in the early Middle Ages. England and Ireland were ruled by the same king by the end of the thirteenth century, but in fact much of Ireland remained completely outside English influence. Relations between England and Ireland have rarely been good, as the Irish have resented English interference with their religious and economic life, while the English have tended to regard the Irish with a mixture of indifference and superiority. England and Scotland came under one king when James VI of Scotland ascended the English throne in 1603, though the Act of Union, which abolished the Scottish Parliament, was not passed until 1707. The Scots retained their legal system, schools and local government structure. In 1800 the Irish Parliament was discontinued and Ireland, like Scotland, was ruled from Westminster. After years of bitter struggle the twenty-six counties of Southern

3

Ireland became independent in 1922, though the six northern counties, which had a Protestant majority, remained part of the United Kingdom. Northern Ireland had its own Parliament at Stormont in Belfast, but in 1972, following several years of grave unrest, this Parliament was suspended and direct rule was imposed from Westminster. (See Chapter 11 for a brief account of the relations between England and Ireland.)

Both Wales and Scotland have nationalist movements, but since the mid-1970s their influence has declined (in the 1974 election 14 Nationalist MPs were returned; in 1983 there were only 4), while in 1979 a proposal to 'devolve' certain government functions in both Scotland and Wales failed to receive the necessary support in referendums held in both countries.

Following the Second World War there were those who felt that the future of Britain lay with Europe. In spite of active campaigning, however, they were unable to convince the politicians who were in power (or, the evidence suggests, the people of Britain), and when the European Economic Community (the EEC) was established Britain remained outside. By the early 1960s opinions had changed, among the government of the day at least, and the United Kingdom applied for membership of the EEC. Negotiations followed, but in 1963 British entry was vetoed by President de Gaulle. The application was renewed in 1967, but very little progress was made until 1970 when detailed discussions got under way. The Treaty of Accession was signed in early 1972 and Britain formally became a member of the Community in January 1973. The terms of accession were attacked by the Labour Party (even though they had been responsible for reopening negotiations in 1967) and they announced that if they were returned to power they would 'renegotiate' the terms of entry and then hold a referendum on the question of membership. In February 1974 the Labour Party won the election and talks commenced shortly afterwards with Britain's Common Market colleagues. These talks continued until late spring 1975 and in June of that year Britain's first referendum took place. Opposing continuing membership of the EEC were many members of the Labour Party, some Conservatives, the Nationalist parties and the Trades Union Congress (the TUC); in favour were a majority of members of the Government, the Conservative leadership and most of the rank and file membership, and the majority of British industrialists and business interests. The referendum was held on 5 June; 17,378,581 votes (67.2 per cent of those

4

cast) were in favour of Britain remaining in the EEC, 8,470,073 votes (32.8 per cent were in favour of leaving the Community. Following the declaration of the result, many of those who had supported the anti-Common Market line announced they would accept the decision, including the TUC and most of the Labour ministers who had spoken against continued membership.

On 14 June 1984 Britain elected 81 representatives to sit in the European Parliament: 66 from England, 8 from Scotland and 4 from Wales by means of the 'first past the post' system as used in UK elections, and 3 from Northern Ireland, by the single transferable vote. The Conservative Party won 45 of the seats and the Labour Party won a further 32, the remaining 4 were won by a Scottish Nationalist, a Democratic Unionist, an Ulster Unionist and a member of the Northern Ireland Social Democratic and Labour Party.

2

The System of Government in Britain

The British system of government is the product of centuries of development that has followed no precise pattern or rigid lines, but rather a course of trial and error. This has at times led to passionate disagreements and bitter feuds, and on some occasions to open conflict. As Britain has no written constitution and relies on a mixture of statute law, common law and conventions (that is, practices and precepts that although not part of a legal code are nevertheless generally accepted), the system of government has remained flexible. Sometimes the system has appeared to be too flexible and different interpretations of the role of certain institutions have been possible at different periods of time. Thus one will find no exact definition of the duties and powers of the British Head of State, beyond the fact that Britain is a monarchy. In theory the monarch's powers appear to be as absolute as they were during the Middle Ages, but in practice this power is restricted in a number of ways.

The system of government that exists in Britain today can perhaps be best described as a mixed governmental system, with the monarch seeming to be, and Parliament in fact being, the senior partner. The monarchy is hereditary, and so when a king or queen dies he or she is automatically succeeded by the next in line. Membership of the House of Lords is largely hereditary, too, although there are also various categories of life peers. The lower house, the House of Commons, is however elected by the British people, and thus represents, or is claimed to represent, their wishes. Over the centuries the Crown and the Lords, that is the hereditary elements of the system, have gradually lost power to the Commons, the representatives of the people.

6

The monarchy

The British have always been ruled by a monarch, except for a brief period during the seventeenth century, and even then the royal line was restored in 1660 shortly after the death of Oliver Cromwell, the Lord Protector. Thus the present sovereign, Elizabeth II, can claim an unbroken descent dating back to the Saxon kings, while other ancestors include Charlemagne, Malcolm II of Scotland and the Emperor Barbarossa. Nevertheless, the succession has not always passed peacefully to the next in line and there are claimants to the throne today who base their case on descent from the Stuarts, who were driven from power in 1688. But there is little danger that latter-day Jacobites will dethrone the Queen, as in addition to her hereditary right she reigns with the consent of Parliament, as has every monarch since William III.

Those who are opposed to the system of monarchy often start by arguing that the institution is non-democratic, as the monarch is not subject to appointment and dismissal by the people and so can become an autocrat. When it is pointed out that this could not occur in Britain because the powers of the Crown are so limited, a further objection is made: 'Why keep the monarchy if it has no function except a ceremonial one?' To answer this we must look at the Queen's duties and see what in fact her functions are.

The visitor to Britain will not have to be unduly observant to notice evidence of the omnipresence of the Queen. Coins and stamps bear a picture of the Queen's head, the post is carried by the 'Royal' Mail, the ships in the 'Royal' Navy are 'Her Majesty's Ships', while 'Her Majesty's Government' is made up of 'Her Majesty's Ministers' and official letters are sent 'On Her Majesty's Service'. The variety and number of institutions bearing the prefix 'Royal' or 'Her Majesty's' suggests that the power of the monarch is considerable. But it is obvious that the Queen is not able to supervise the activities of even a fraction of them, and it soon becomes evident that such prefixes appear as a synonym for 'State' or 'British' when used in official titles, and do not imply that the Queen is in direct control of all the things that are done in her name. This is in fact the key to the problem: all the actions of government are carried out in the Queen's name, and automatically have her approval, although she has no personal knowledge of them.

The monarch, then, is the personification of the British state. When Louis XIV said (or was reputed to say) 'L'état c'est moi', he was

7

speaking as an absolute monarch. When the twentieth-century British citizen says that his Queen is the personification of the state, he means that she is the symbol of the state. This is the true function of the British monarch today – a symbol – and as such the Queen's functions are virtually all ceremonial. She opens Parliament, but takes no part in its deliberations and is in fact forbidden to enter the chamber of the House of Commons, as all monarchs have been since Charles I in 1641 rashly tried to arrest five Members of whom he disapproved. No Bill can become an Act, that is have the force of law, unless the monarch has approved it, but the power of veto has not been used for more than two centuries, and any attempt to block legislation by its use would precipitate a constitutional crisis of major proportions.

It is in relation to Parliament, however, that the monarch appears to retain real power, for it is the monarch who has the responsibility of choosing the Prime Minister and other government ministers. However, in practice, the Queen must choose the leader of the party which has the majority in the House of Commons. It is the electorate who decide which the largest party will be, and the members of the party who select their leader, and so the Queen's freedom of choice is extremely limited. Once a Prime Minister has been appointed it is he or she who chooses the members of the Government, and these men and women are then presented to the Queen as 'her' ministers.

Until recently the monarch exercised more freedom of action in choosing a Prime Minister, and there have been several occasions this century when the monarch's choice was not the obvious one. In 1923 George V asked Stanley Baldwin to form a government in succession to Bonar Law, when the next in line appeared to be Lord Curzon, the Foreign Secretary. The king thought that in the twentieth century the Prime Minister should sit in the Commons, not the Lords, and accordingly Curzon, to his bitter disappointment, was passed over. Again in 1940 George VI chose Winston Churchill to succeed Neville Chamberlain, when his personal preference was for Lord Halifax, because he felt in wartime the Prime Minister must sit in the Commons. The choice has not always been between a member of the House of Lords and a member of the House of Commons. In 1957 Harold Macmillan became Prime Minister on the retirement of Sir Anthony Eden, when many people thought that R. A. Butler was the stronger candidate. Nor has the Commons always won against the Lords, for in 1963 Lord Home was chosen to succeed Macmillan (the favourite was again Mr Butler) when he was still a member of the

House of Lords. (Lord Home subsequently disclaimed his peerage, see p. 47.)

It now seems clear that should a Prime Minister resign or die while in office, the party to which he or she belonged would insist on electing a new party leader using the procedures established by the party in question, that is, election by MPs in the case of the Conservative Party; by representatives of the unions, of constituencies and the parliamentary Party, in a ratio of 40: 30: 30, for the Labour Party; and by all party members in the case of the Liberal Party and the Social Democratic Party (SDP), who make up the Alliance. The man or woman chosen would then be asked by the monarch to take up the office of Prime Minister. If the Queen exercised her theoretical perogative of choice in defiance of the party's wishes, it is almost certain that the party involved would refuse to accept her candidate. However, following the formation of the Alliance, the possibility of a 'hung Parliament' (with no party having a clear majority) has led to a considerable amount of discussion about the role of the monarch if no party were to have a clear majority. It seems quite possible, writing in early 1986, when the opinion polls suggest that all three party groups have a similar level of support, that a general election result could be, for example, Conservatives 300, Labour 300, Alliance 50, that is, neither of the 'traditional parties' would have a majority. Presumably, both would court the Alliance with offers of ministerial seats and the inclusion of aspects of the Alliance programme in their plans for legislation. While both of the major parties have dismissed any plans for a coalition it seems unlikely that they have not had private discussions among themselves as to what action they should take in the event of a result such as that described above. Indeed, it is also possible that an election would give a result in which one party got more votes than any other, but did not have a majority over all other parties; this, again, could result in a coalition. In such an eventuality, it seems that the monarch would have to wait on discussions between the various political parties in order to see what combination of groups would result and then she would ask the leader of the largest combination to form a Government. There could be difficulties, however, if there was no clear agreement – if, for example, the Alliance, which is itself a coalition between the Liberals and the SDP, split into its two components – the Crown would have to exercise extreme caution to avoid the charge of becoming politically involved. What is certain is that the monarch cannot ask a politician without parliamentary support to become Prime

Minister, as such a person would not be able to form a government, and it is not possible to be a Prime Minister without an administration. In theory, the Queen could ask a member of the House of Lords to form a Government made up of members of the Lords but in practice, as we have seen, it is no longer considered acceptable for a Prime Minister to sit in the Lords, and any such action would lead to an enormous outcry and would probably damage the position of the monarch irreparably.

Another interesting point concerning the monarch's powers is the question of the dissolution of Parliament. Parliament is dissolved by the monarch but can only be dissolved with its own consent. Opinions differ as to whether the monarch is bound to give the Prime Minister a dissolution just because he or she asks for one. It is thought to be legitimate for prime ministers to ask for a dissolution if they feel that they do not have a large enough majority to allow the Government to carry on its business, as Harold Wilson did in 1966, when his majority was three, and again in 1974 when he was the head of a minority Government. However, if a Prime Minister asked for a dissolution for a frivolous reason, or when the opposition parties were split to such an extent that they could not provide an alternative Government, it is possible that the monarch would refuse to grant the request. But in the latter case, if the Prime Minister refused to continue and no other member of the party agreed to form an administration, and if any of the opposition parties were completely incapable of forming a Government, the result would probably be chaos and a dissolution. The whole process would undoubtedly do much to discredit Parliament and the cry would go up that the Crown was being involved in politics.

Politics in this context means, of course, party politics, with the implication that the Crown would be called upon to express a preference for one party rather than another. In the past monarchs were often blatant in their support for one party (or one politician) rather than another, but in modern times the monarch has been expected to be completely neutral as far as parties and personalities are concerned. (It is generally acknowledged that Queen Victoria detested the Liberal leader W. E. Gladstone and distrusted his party, but nevertheless she was compelled to accept him as her Prime Minister on no less than four occasions.) At the present time a Labour Government is as acceptable to the Crown as a Conservative Government (or indeed any other government). As we have seen the Government is Her Majesty's Government and the ministers are Her Majesty's Ministers, taking their office from the Crown. The relationship of the Opposition to the

Crown is also acknowledged by the fact that it is termed Her Majesty's Opposition. Between 1945 and the late seventies it was generally agreed that Britain had a 'two party' system of parliamentary government, one party, either the Conservative or Labour Party, formed the Government, while the other formed the Opposition. The rump of the Liberal Party was considered to be insignificant in party terms. In the eighties the formation of the Alliance, made up of Liberals and Social Democrats (many of whom are former right-wing members of the Labour Party), has prompted many commentators to suggest that Britain now has a three party system. However, at the present time there is still only one official Opposition headed by the Leader of the Opposition and paid a salary in respect of this position (see also p. 15). Thus although the Government and the Opposition may oppose each other's philosophies and policies they both owe loyalty to the Crown which represents the British constitutional system. The point is further underlined if one considers the membership of the Privy Council, the body entrusted with the duty of proffering advice to the monarch (see also p. 13). The leaders and many of the senior members of both the government and opposition parties are Privy Councillors, along with other distinguished personages of varied political affiliation (or none at all).

This lack of political involvement can have some curious side effects. Each session of Parliament opens with the Queen's Speech, which contains details of the Government's programme for the session. Thus if a Labour Government was in power the Speech might propose legislation for nationalisation and increased state intervention in the planning of the economy. The next year a change of political fortune at the polls might mean that the Queen's Speech contained a Conservative programme to denationalise industry and reduce state intervention.

While the Queen undoubtedly has private views she must ensure that they remain private; on virtually every controversial issue the Queen and other members of the royal family have to maintain a discreet silence. If the Queen makes a public statement she does so on the advice of her ministers, and the statement will have been prepared by them. Just as ministers are expected to advise the monarch on controversial matters, so the monarch has the right to advise ministers and it is probably here that the monarchy retains the last of its political power. The monarch is, except in the rare event of abdication, on the throne for life, whereas ministers have a much shorter tenure of office.

11

Over the years a monarch can build up a great deal of experience in government, because each day state papers and other important documents are delivered to the palace, for perusal by the Queen in her capacity as Head of State. She also holds regular audiences for the Prime Minister and other ministers, who are expected to tell her what is happening in their departments and in the Government as a whole. Queen Victoria, who came to the throne in 1837 and died in 1901, accumulated a considerable amount of expertise about the constitutional process, and was only too willing to proffer advice to her ministers.

A question that has received considerable attention in recent years is whether the monarchy is too expensive. In 1952 when Queen Elizabeth II ascended the throne Parliament debated the question of the Civil List and agreed to grant the Queen an annual sum of £475,000. The greater part of the Civil List was earmarked for household expenses and salaries of members of the household, though £95,000 was a supplementary provision to take care of inflation. In January 1972 the Civil List was revised and under the new arrangements the Queen received £980,000; by 1984 this had risen to £3.85 million. The Civil List is free from income tax, although the Queen pays tax on income from her private estates. Certain other members of the royal family also receive allowances from the state but the Prince of Wales, the heir to the throne, does not – his income comes from the Duchy of Cornwall.

The Queen is granted the Civil List in return for handing over the Crown Estates to the Exchequer, and this has happened since the time of George III. Although the Crown Estates officially belong to the Crown no monarch could keep them if for some reason he or she considered that the Civil List was inadequate. By convention the monarch hands over the Estates, and convention in this context has virtual force of law. Nor do the Crown Estates belong to the monarch as personal property, for most of them date from the time, still preserved in the usage 'Royal' and 'Her Majesty's', when the state and Crown were almost indistinguishable.

Nevertheless, the Queen has a considerable personal fortune, in addition to jewels, paintings and a stamp collection that is said to be worth over a million pounds. She owns two of the royal residences, Balmoral and Sandringham (when Edward VIII abdicated in 1936 his brother, who became George VI, had to buy them from him), though Buckingham Palace and other royal palaces, such as Windsor Castle and Holyrood House in Scotland, are maintained by the state. The state also pays for the Queen's aircraft, maintained by the Royal Air Force, the Royal Yacht, which is part of the Royal Navy, and various administrative expenses.

In return for the royal salary, for that is what the Civil List amounts to, the Queen is expected to fulfil her constitutional duties and also to undertake tours and visits in Britain, the Commonwealth and foreign countries. It is in this area that the Queen and her family have a very important role to play, for the British royal family enjoys considerable prestige, both at home and overseas. People seem to be attracted by the aura of monarchy and the glamour that accompanies it. There is little doubt that the royal family is a great tourist attraction, and Buckingham Palace is an object of pilgrimage for many visitors to Britain, particularly for those staunch republicans, the Americans.

The glamour of monarchy is also seen in its connections with the House of Lords and the orders and decorations that are granted in the royal name. Britain is one of the few countries where the aristocracy retains a certain amount of political power, and the Crown's role in the maintenance of this power is of considerable importance. In earlier times the monarch enjoyed the right to give titles to anyone he or she liked, and a number of the present members of the House of Lords owe their seats to the fact that one of their ancestors was a sovereign's favourite. Today, peers are created on the advice of the Prime Minister who will also consult the leaders of the other main political parties. The Queen is also responsible for all other honours that are given in her name, such as knighthoods and the membership of various orders, though once again these are given largely on political advice. There are, however, one or two orders that are reserved for those who have given special services to the sovereign.

It can be argued that the monarchy, because of its close connection with the aristocracy and its aloofness from everyday life, contributes to social divisions within society, but few people in Britain seem to be in favour of its abolition. If a newspaper article or book is published that is even mildly critical of the royal family, there is an outcry, and all kinds of terrible punishments, from incarceration in the Tower of London downwards, are suggested for the unfortunate author.

The Privy Council

It is the Privy Council's duty to offer advice to the monarch, and it is through the Council that he or she exercises statutory powers. In addition to having this advisory function the Privy Council also discharges certain other duties not directly concerned with the monarch.

Today its functions are almost completely ceremonial, though it is considered a great honour to be invited to become a Privy Councillor. All Cabinet Ministers receive the title on assuming office for the first time, and distinguished public figures from Britain and the Commonwealth are invited to become Councillors on the recommendation of the Prime Minister. Membership of the Council is for life, and there are usually about 300 Councillors at any one time, all of whom are entitled to be called 'The Right Honourable . . . ', and put the letters PC after their names.

The Council is presided over by the monarch (or in the absence of the monarch, by Counsellors of State). Officially a quorum is three, although in practice meetings are rarely attended by fewer than four Councillors. The Council only meets as a whole on important occasions such as when the sovereign dies.

The Privy Council has a number of committees, and it is out of these in the past that departments of state have grown, for example, the Department of Education and Science. The most important committee of the Privy Council today is the Judicial Committee and there are also committees concerned with the Channel Islands, the Isle of Man, the universities of Oxford and Cambridge, the Scottish universities, the granting of charters to municipal corporations, and the baronetage.

Parliament

The British Parliament consists of a lower chamber, the House of Commons, and an upper chamber, the House of Lords. It sits in the Palace of Westminster – probably better known as the Houses of Parliament – which is situated between Westminster Abbey and the River Thames.

Parliament has the following responsibilities: it passes legislation, it provides the finance necessary for the running of the state, and it brings forward important issues for discussion by the Commons, or the Lords, or both. It also ratifies international treaties and agreements to which Britain becomes a party, although in theory the making of treaties is the prerogative of the sovereign. Parliament is, in short, responsible for governing the country, and this government is carried on by agreement between the political parties elected to the House of

Commons by the citizens of the United Kingdom. The majority party forms the Government and the largest minority party the Opposition. Thus the minority parties accept the right of the majority party to run the country, while the majority party accepts the right of the minority parties to criticise the way this is being done. Without this tacit agreement between the political parties, the British parliamentary system would break down. It is also important to realise that the Opposition is an alternative Government and its members are potential ministers.

As we have seen there are some who claim that Britain's traditional two party system has broken down so that it is no longer possible to argue that there are clear cut government and opposition parties, nevertheless power will ultimately depend on the number of MPs each of the competing parties has following a general election.

Members of the House of Commons are chosen by the people, at elections, but members of the House of Lords sit by right, as peers of the realm. To be passed by Parliament a Bill must go through both Houses, and then it must be approved by the monarch before it can become law. The details of this process will be discussed on pp. 33–41.

The two Houses of Parliament are responsible for arranging their own affairs, free from interference from the Crown, or any other outside body, and these privileges, won over the centuries with great difficulty, are jealously guarded. Ultimately who sits in the Commons is decided by the electorate and each Member of Parliament is responsible to the voters of his or her own constituency. However, Members of Parliament are not delegates, but representatives, that is, they do not have to put into force a policy that has been decided by the people who have chosen them. As representatives they can act as they think fit, only being accountable for their stewardship at elections. There have always been those who feel that MPs should be more closely answerable to the views and opinions of the electorate and, on occasion, steps have been taken to bring pressure on the Members concerned.

Indeed, the current situation in the Labour Party is that Members of Parliament must apply for reselection. When this system was introduced there were those who feared that many sitting Members would be 'deselected' by small extremist groups within constituency parties but, in practice, most of the sitting Members were confirmed.

Until the referendum of June 1975 there was no provision under the British system of government for any form of direct democracy. The decision to hold a referendum caused disquiet among some MPs because they felt that it would undermine the powers of Parliament. In the event the voters supported Parliament's decision on EEC membership and so no conflict arose. It is, however, interesting to note that since June 1975 suggestions have been put forward for national referendums on other issues. As yet, none of these has been taken up though in 1979 Scotland and Wales held referendums on the issue of devolution (see p. 21). Voters, of course, have the right of direct access to their MP and can bring matters of importance to his or her notice. In this way the individual Member of Parliament is the vital link between the citizens and government.

THE POLITICAL PARTIES
The British electorate choose their representatives in Parliament at 'general elections' or 'by-elections'. At the former all parliamentary seats are contested, and there must be a general election at least every five years. A by-election occurs when a seat in Parliament falls vacant, owing to the death or 'resignation' of a Member and an election is held to select a new Member for that particular seat. In theory electors vote for an individual, and for many years the ballot paper on which people recorded their vote made no mention of political parties. In fact most people seem to vote for the candidates of one of the political parties, and the majority of the electorate until recently saw the choice as lying between two parties, Labour and Conservative.

However, at the 1983 general election Members of Parliament representing eleven different parties were returned, though the Labour and Conservative parties won far more seats than any other party – Labour had 209 seats and the Conservatives 397 (which gave them the largest majority since the Second World War). The next largest party was the Liberal Party with 17 seats, while their allies the Social Democratic Party won 6. The Scottish Nationalist Party and the Welsh Nationalist Party (Plaid Cymru) had both enjoyed considerable success in the 1970s (in the 1974 election the former had won 11 seats), but by 1983 there were only 2 Members from each of these parties. The balance of the 650 Members came from the Province of Northern Ireland which returned a total of 17 Members – 11 Ulster Unionists, 3 Democratic Unionists, and 1 each from the Ulster Popular Unionist Party, the Social Democratic and Labour Party, and Sinn Fein. It is the policy of the last-named party not to take up any seats at Westminster as they are bitterly opposed to what they consider to be Britain's 'occupation' of Ulster (see pp. 148–53).

Although the Conservative Party won an overall majority of 144 over all other parties, they got into office on a minority of the votes cast: while 42·4 per cent of the electorate voted for Mrs Thatcher and her colleagues, 57·6 per cent voted against them. Another interesting feature of the 1983 election was that in percentage terms the voting for the Labour Party and the SDP/Liberal Alliance was very close: 27·6 per cent for Labour and 25·4 per cent for the Alliance, the result in the number of seats, however, was 209 as opposed to 23!

The reason why the Conservative and Labour parties have such a large number of seats compared with the other parties can be found in the voting system, which we shall examine shortly (see p. 25).

The Conservative and Liberal parties can trace their origins back to the Tories and Whigs of the seventeenth century, but it is only comparatively recently that the modern parties, with their elaborate bureaucracies of paid organisers and agents, have developed. Until the last years of the nineteenth century the Conservatives and Liberals were the only parties elected on a national basis to the House of Commons (there were a number of Irish Nationalists sitting for Irish seats, but they were primarily concerned with Irish affairs). In 1867, 1884 and 1885, working-class men were given the vote and in the 1890s a number of socialists were returned. By the first decade of the twentieth century the Labour Party had become a significant force in British politics. During the interwar period the Labour Party displaced the Liberals as the second party in Parliament, though quite a sizeable Liberal 'rump' persisted up until the Second World War.

In 1945, following the end of hostilities in Europe, an election was held which was won by the Labour Party, by 393 seats to the Conservatives' 213. The Liberal Party was reduced to a mere 12 seats. The 1950 election resulted in another Labour victory, although with a much reduced majority, and the following year the Conservatives were returned to power. The Conservatives won the 1956 and 1959 elections, but they were turned out in 1964 by the Labour Party which won with a majority of 3 seats over all other parties. In 1966 a further election was held which gave the Labour Party a majority of 96. Four years later it was the turn of the Conservatives, who won by 30 seats, and they held office until February 1974, when the Labour Party became the largest single party in the House of Commons, with 301 seats. If the Conservatives (296 seats) had been able to do a deal with the Liberals (14 seats), they could have formed a coalition which would have given them a majority over the Labour Party. But the Liberals were unwilling to ally themselves with the Conservatives and the Labour leader, Harold Wilson, formed a Government. Running the country with a minority Government proved to be extremely difficult, and in October a new election was held. In this election the Labour Party gained a majority of 3 seats over all other parties.

Harold Wilson led the Government until 1976 when he handed over to James Callaghan who had been serving as Foreign Secretary. With a majority of only 3 Callaghan found that he had considerable difficulty in getting legislation through the House and so an agreement was reached with the Liberal Party, the 'Lib–Lab pact', whereby the Liberal MPs, although not entering into a formal coalition with the Government, agreed to support it in the voting lobbies. In 1979, however, Mr Callaghan lost a vote of confidence and the Government resigned. The Conservatives won the ensuing general election and Mrs Thatcher became the country's first woman Prime Minister. The first eighteen months of the Thatcher government were difficult as Britain, along with the rest of the Western world, was suffering from a severe trade recession. Seeing as their number one priority the reduction of inflation, the Conservatives adopted policies aimed at cutting public spending and increasing Britain's competitiveness in world markets. An immediate result was a considerable increase in unemployment and by 1982 the Conservative government, and the Prime Minister in particular, were experiencing extremely poor results in the opinion polls. In April 1982, however, the Argentinians invaded the Falkland Islands and the government mounted an immediate operation to recapture them. The switch in public opinion was instantaneous and when the British forces marched into Port Stanley, capital of the Falklands, in June, Mrs Thatcher was riding high in popular esteem, a position she maintained into the election in May the following year which she won with a large majority (see p. 26).

The Conservative Party can loosely be described as the party of the middle and upper classes, the party of the property-owner and the businessman. Much of the money used for financing party campaigns, at both local and national level, comes from large industrial concerns, and many Conservative MPs sit on the boards of leading companies. However, a number of studies have shown that a substantial number of the working class consistently vote Conservative. The reasons for this are not entirely clear, but it has been suggested that in some cases people have improved their social position to some extent, and voting Conservative is one way of demonstrating this. Others, it is thought, vote Conservative because they feel that Conservatives are 'gentlemen' and as such have a better understanding of the way government works. This attitude seems to be found mainly in country areas. The Conservatives draw most of their support from rural areas, small towns and the residential suburbs of large cities.

The Labour Party has always had strong links with the trade union movement and much of its financial backing comes from this source. Some unions nominate candidates for particular seats, making themselves responsible for electoral and other expenses. This support is of considerable importance to the party, as for obvious reasons they cannot rely on assistance from large industrial combines.

The Labour Party draws most of its support from the working class, but also attracts votes from certain sections of the middle class and a core of intellectuals who are regarded with considerable distrust by some party members. The traditional Labour voter, however, is the industrial worker, who is also a trade unionist. The Labour Party is strongest in industrial areas and the towns.

At one time the second large party in Parliament was the Liberal Party. During the twentieth century, however, it has been replaced by the Labour Party, for while the Conservatives seem to have been able to adapt to changing circumstances, the Liberals appear unable to find a role in modern conditions. After an impressive start in the Liberal administration of 1906 to 1916, the party virtually tore itself apart during and after the First World War. Even so, the Liberal Party has not disappeared completely, and according to some optimists the Liberal revival is merely a matter of time. However, their progress has been painfully slow. At the beginning of the 1960s the Liberals had only 6 seats in Parliament, although in 1962 against all expectations they won a by-election in Orpington. In the general election of 1964 their representation had grown to 9 seats, but was only 14 ten years later, a disheartening result when one takes into account that they won over 18 per cent of the popular vote. In 1981 a new force arrived in British political life in the shape of the Social Democratic Party (the SDP) formed by Labour politicians out of sympathy with Labour Party policies (they were subsequently joined by a solitary Conservative MP). The SDP was launched on a great wave of popular support that was consolidated by spectacular by-election victories at Crosby in Lancashire and Hillhead in Glasgow, while a Liberal with SDP support won in Croydon. For a short time it looked as if the Liberals and the SDP, joined in an electoral alliance, would carry all before them, but a combination of events, including the Falklands War and the reluctance of many to support the link between Liberals and the SDP led to a decline in the backing for the 'Third Force'. In the 1983 election only 6 SDP Members and 17 Liberals were returned to the House of Commons. Shortly after the election the SDP leader, Roy Jenkins, resigned to be replaced by Dr David Owen who had at one time held office as a Labour Foreign Secretary.

After discussions the Liberals and the SDP agreed that the formal Alliance would continue and between the election of 1983 and May 1986 they won three by-elections, at Portsmouth, Brecon and Ryedale. According to the Labour and Conservative parties the Alliance draws much of its electoral support from 'protest voters'. They claim that such people will support the Alliance at by-elections, but return to their traditional voting patterns when a general election is held. However, some political commentators say that while there is some evidence of this, there are also strong indications that in fact the policies put forward by the Alliance have a strong appeal to those who feel disinclined to support what they regard as the more extreme policies of the Conservative or Labour parties.

The dominant party in Northern Ireland is that of the Ulster Unionists and 11 of the province's MPs elected in 1983 belong to the party. There are also 3 Democratic Unionists and 1 Ulster Popular Unionist. All the Unionist parties favour the maintenance of the links between Northern Ireland and the rest of the United Kingdom and fervently oppose any attempt to unite Ulster and the Republic of Ireland. At one time, the Unionists were closely affiliated with the Conservative Party but the troubles that have afflicted Northern Ireland since 1969 have led to a breach between the Conservatives and the various branches of the Unionist camp. Two other party groups from Northern Ireland have elected members – the Social Democratic and Labour Party and one from Sinn Fein – although the latter refuses to take his seat at Westminster. (In January 1986 one of the Ulster Unionists lost his seat to a Social Democratic and Labour Party member.)

Of considerable interest in recent years has been the fluctuating fortunes of the Nationalist parties. Although Plaid Cymru (the Welsh Nationalists) and the Scottish Nationalist Party regularly put candidates up for Parliament, during the 1950s and 1960s they rarely attracted many votes. However, in the early 1970s support increased and in the election of October 1974 the Scottish Nationalists won 11 seats while their Welsh counterparts won 3. This, however, represented the high spot of their achievement. In 1975 the government announced that limited devolution, a transfer of powers stopping short of self-government would be introduced for Scotland and Wales and in 1979 referendums were held in both countries to gauge the popular mood towards the proposals. It was agreed before the vote was taken that the devolution proposals would only be put into effect if 40 per cent of the electorate supported the measures. In the event, only 12 per cent of the Welsh electorate and 33 per cent of the Scottish electorate voted in favour of the proposals and the Government concluded that this did not justify the introduction of devolution. As a result, the Nationalist parties withdrew their support from the Prime Minister, James Callaghan – an action that led to his defeat on a motion of no confidence in March 1979 and his subsequent defeat at the polls two months later. Ironically, the ensuing election proved disastrous for the Nationalists: they lost 10 of their 14 seats, leaving the Scottish Nationalists with 2 seats against the 11 they had previously held, and Plaid Cymru with 2 as opposed to the 3 they represented before the election was called. This pattern was repeated at the 1983 election.

THE HOUSE OF COMMONS
Elections The members of the House of Commons (Members of Parliament) are elected by those of their fellow citizens who have attained the age of 18, and who are not specifically disqualified from voting by law (see p. 22). General elections must take place at least every five years, though there is no fixed date on which an election must be held. In practice the choice of the election date almost invariably rests with the Prime Minister of the day, and it is obvious that he or she will choose a time that will give his or her party the maximum advantage. As we have seen, a Prime Minister with a valid reason for a dissolution (and valid reasons are not difficult to find) would encounter no difficulty from the monarch, so within the limits of the five-year rule a Prime Minister has considerable scope for manoeuvre. One factor that may restrict this freedom of action is the size of the Government's majority, for the inability to carry through a legislative programme can bring down a Government more quickly than anything else. Given a reasonable majority, however, a Government can put itself in a strong position when a general election is due. Apart from the

great advantage of selecting the date, the Government can arrange its legislation in such a way that the period immediately before an election sees measures that will make the administration popular with the voters. There is of course the danger that if the Government is too generous the Opposition parties will immediately suspect that the thoughts of the Prime Minister are turning towards the ballot box. Indeed, by the time a Government enters its fourth year, parliamentarians, political commentators and the general public are all keeping a close eye on events in the hope of finding out when the next election will occur.

Once the Prime Minister has decided that the time has come for an election the monarch is asked for a dissolution and Parliament is then terminated by Royal Proclamation. Polling day is seventeen working days from the date of dissolution. As soon as Parliament has been dissolved the Lord Chancellor issues writs for the holding of fresh elections throughout the country, and these writs are sent to the returning officers in each parliamentary constituency. In urban constituencies the returning officer is the chairman of the district council, in rural constituencies the sheriff of the county performs the duties of the office. In Scotland the appropriate officer is the sheriff and in Northern Ireland, the under-sheriff. The returning officer appoints a deputy returning officer, usually the clerk of the council, and it is this official who actually arranges the election. Details of arrangements for the election must be published by the returning officer by 4 p.m. the day after the writs have been issued.

The election is now formally under way and all those concerned in it have been informed of the fact. The most important participants are, of course, the voters who are actually responsible for choosing the MP. Each constituency has a register of voters and this is brought up to date in November of each year. This enables new electors to be entered on the register, while people who are no longer resident in the constituency have their names removed, for the vote depends on residence, that is, everybody votes in the constituency in which he or she lives. Until 1948 some people had two votes; if they lived in one constituency and had business premises elsewhere they were entitled to a business vote, while graduates of the older universities could vote for 'university seats'. These forms of voting were abolished by the Representation of the People Act of 1948, and so it is only from this date that Britain has fully accepted the principle of 'one person, one vote'. Even today there are a few exceptions to this principle. Apart from those under 18 years of age, peers and peeresses in their own right, persons of 'unsound mind' and felons (those serving criminal sentences of more than twelve months) are not allowed to vote. Also excluded are people who have been involved in electoral offences. People who are away from home on polling day, or who are serving overseas in an official capacity, can make arrangements to vote by post or proxy.

A constituency usually consists of about 60,000 voters, although as the population may change from one election to the next there is a Boundary Commission, which constantly reviews constituency boundaries and recommends adjustments when necessary. Thus constituencies may disappear or alter in size, while entirely new seats may be created, and these changes may also produce a change in voting patterns. In 1986 there were 523 constituencies in England, 38 in Wales, 72 in Scotland and 17 in Northern Ireland.

If the electors are the most important actors in the election drama, next in order of importance are the candidates. Any man or woman over 21 can be a candidate at a parliamentary election, with the following exceptions: peers and peeresses in their own right, lunatics, felons and those who have committed electoral offences, that is, the same categories as those excluded from voting, with the following additions: clergymen of the Church of England or the Roman Catholic Church, undischarged bankrupts and those holding 'offices of profit under the Crown'. The last includes civil servants and members of the armed forces; if they wish to stand for Parliament they must first resign from their posts.

Once he has decided to stand, the prospective candidate must fill in nomination papers, which contain his or her full name and occupation, and these are then signed by a proposer, a seconder and eight other electors for the constituency in which the candidate is standing. The nomination form must be handed in to the returning officer not later than the eighth day after the proclamation summoning the new Parliament. The Candidate must also produce a deposit of £500 which is lost if the candidate receives less than 5 per cent of the votes cast. The purpose of this deposit is to discourage frivolous candidatures.

Once candidates have declared themselves they have to convince the voters that they are the best person to be their MP, and indeed if they are wise they will have been doing so for some time before the election. As has already been pointed out, virtually all the seats at a general election are fought on a party basis. The candidates are selected by the local party organisation, and are then supported by this organisation in their fight for the seat. Both of the major parties have a branch in nearly every constituency while the Alliance parties also have local branches established by either the Liberal or Social Democratic Party; though their coverage is not as comprehensive as the larger parties. If the candidate wins the seat the local party continues its support, often providing an office where constituents can be interviewed, and secretarial assistance. In both main parties the local parties are responsible for the selection of candidates, although the central organisation can intervene if it considers that the choice is totally unsuitable or damaging to the party's prospects. The local parties, however, guard their independence jealously and central interference is relatively rare. In most cases the local constituency party supplies the candidate with an agent, and it is this person's responsibility to direct the election campaign in that partiuclar constituency. Some wealthy constituency organisations have salaried full-time agents. Those that are less well off rely on a part-time agent, or someone recruited for the period of the election. The agent arranges meetings at which the candidate can meet the public and get both policies and personality over. The agent is also responsible for arranging 'canvassing', the backbone of election work, which consists of the candidate and helpers knocking on doors and asking the voters for their support. There is a certain amount of disagreement over how effective canvassing is, but there are few agents who would have the courage to suggest that it is unnecessary. Another important duty of the agent is to keep an eye on expenditure, to ensure that election expenses do not exceed the legal limit, which is £2,700 plus 2·3 pence for each elector in a borough constituency and £2,700 plus 3·1 pence in a county constituency.

The local party is greatly helped if its candidate has been the MP for the constituency in the previous Parliament. Even if he or she has not been particularly effective, the candidate's name will probably be better known than those of any opponents, who might well have visited the constituency for the first time on the evening of their adoption meeting. (Candidates do not have to live in the constituency they stand for, though many buy or rent a house there if they are elected.)

Studies have shown that at national elections people tend to vote for a party rather than a person, and therefore it is important that the candidate is identified with the party for which he or she is standing. It has been estimated that when all the candidates are standing for the first time in a constituency, their individual characteristics only make a difference of a few hundred votes. Of course, a few hundred votes can be of great importance in the simple majority vote system, as is illustrated by the following example from Caithness and Sutherland (Scotland) in the 1945 election:

E. L. Gander Dower	(C)	5,564
R. McInnes	(Lab)	5,558
A. Sinclair	(Lib)	5,503
Conservative majority		6

The Conservative was elected, even though the Labour candidate received almost as many votes as he did. If the Labour and Liberal votes are added together it will be seen that nearly twice as many people voted against the Conservative as voted for him. It is an interesting feature of the British system that it is not uncommon for an MP to represent a constituency in which more people have voted against than have voted for him or her though the results are not always as dramatic as in the example given above.

Another disadvantage of the majority vote is that it does not accurately reflect the wishes of the electorate as a whole, as a party can win a larger share of the popular vote than its opponents, but still end up with fewer seats. This is due to the fact that in many constituencies a large number of votes are 'wasted': a candidate returned with a majority of one is just as much a Member of Parliament as a candidate who gets a majority of 20,000. Another feature of the present system is that a small party may get a large number of votes at a general election in the country as a whole but the voters will be spread out over more than 600 constituencies and therefore the number of seats actually won will be out of proportion to the support they can muster. These points are illustrated by the election results for 1951, February 1974 and May 1983.

In 1951, although the Labour Party received more votes than the Conservatives, the Conservatives won more seats:

	Votes	*Seats*	*% of votes*
Conservative	13,717,538	321	48·0
Labour	13,948,605	295	48·8
Liberal	730,556	6	2·5
Others	198,969	–	0·7

Thus the Conservatives formed the Government.

In February 1974, however, the result was:

	Votes	Seats	% of votes
Labour	11,661,488	301	37·2
Conservative	11,928,677	296	38·1
Liberal	6,056,713	14	19·3
Others	1,695,315	23	5·4

In this case the Labour Party won fewer votes than the Conservatives, but 5 more seats. There were also 36 MPs who belonged to neither the Conservative Party nor the Labour Party. (The 37th 'other' was the Speaker.) For a few days it was far from clear what was going to happen. While the commentators discussed the pros and cons of minority governments and coalitions, the politicians vied with one another to give their interpretation of the electorate's wishes. It was only after the Liberals rejected the idea of entering a coalition with the Conservatives that Edward Heath, the Conservative Prime Minister who had called the election, decided to resign, giving up the seals of office to Harold Wilson.

In May 1983 Mrs Thatcher was returned to power with a massive majority in House of Commons seats, though an analysis of the popular vote shows that again more people opposed the government than supported it:

	Votes	Seats	% of votes
Conservative	13,012,612	397	42·4
Labour	8,456,504	209	27·6
SDP/Liberal Alliance	7,793,778	17	25·4
Others	1,420,590	21	4·6

It is because of results like these that there has been increasing pressure in recent years for a change in the electoral system. It has been argued that the great advantage of the British 'first past the post' system was that it gives greater stability – in the twenty-three elections held in the present century eighteen produced an overall majority. It is interesting to compare this with Finland, a country where elections are conducted on the proportional representation system, where half the governments since independence in 1917 have not enjoyed majority support. Since the Second World War the average length of a Finnish Government has been just over twelve months, in

Britain during the same period the average has been three years and five months.

Not surprisingly, the most eloquent supporters of the proportional representation system of voting come from the smaller parties, particularly the Liberals and the SDP. Critics of the system suggest that, in practice, proportional representation is no more democratic than the majority vote, as it rarely returns a party large enough to form a Government on its own. Thus a coalition must be established, and as a coalition usually means a compromise on policy members of a coalition may have difficulty in fulfilling their election programme. Other critics point out that one of the strengths of the British parliamentary system is that MPs are elected by specific geographical constituencies and on election are expected to represent the interests of all their electorate, whatever their political inclination. However, it is clear that the debate on the most appropriate electoral system will continue and that if the Alliance are in a position to hold the balance of power at a general election they will regard the issue of electoral reform as being a key factor in deciding which of the major parties to support. It is equally clear that neither the Conservative nor Labour parties are inclined to change the present system as, as has been shown in the election results quoted, it clearly benefits the 'two party system'. If proportional representation were introduced, and the Labour Party and the Alliance were to win a similar share of the popular vote this would mean they would have a far more equal share of the MPs in the House, and few Labour Members would welcome that. Nor is there reason to believe that the Alliance would take seats only from Labour because since 1981 they have taken six seats from the Conservatives in by-elections.

Until recently it was an interesting feature of British elections that relatively few voters changed their opinions from one general election to the next, and indeed most seemed to vote consistently for one party all their adult life. As we have seen some commentators believe that this pattern is changing and that radical changes are taking place in British political life. Certainly it is the aim of all the political parties to convince the voter that it is their policies that are most appropriate for the needs of the country, and each of the parties produces a great variety of propaganda at election time. Virtually all the parties issue an election manifesto which lays down their aims and policies and these are discussed and quoted at great length during the campaign at public meetings, on radio and television and in the press. Each candidate also prepares an election address, which is distributed to each voter in his or her constituency, and consists of a localised version of the party's manifesto, together with questions of particular interest to that constituency.

The whole national campaign comes to a head on polling day, which is customarily a Thursday. Polling booths are open from 7 a.m. until 10 p.m.; but polling day is not a holiday, so workers have to vote on the way to work, or in the evening. After all the votes are cast they are counted by tellers, and the result is then announced by the returning officer. Interest is usually concentrated on 'marginal seats', i.e. those that are most likely to change hands. A seat like the Rhondda in South Wales, with a Labour majority of 21,370 in May 1983, is almost certain to remain Labour, while there seems little chance that Christchurch (Conservative majority of 19,738 in 1983) will ever return an MP of a party other than Conservative. Each party has a number of these 'safe' seats; it is the 'marginals' that can go either way, and these decide the result of the election.

Formation of the Government   Once the election is over the monarch calls upon the leader of the victorious party to form a Government. Having accepted the invitation, the new Prime Minister goes to his or her official residence, 10 Downing Street (given by George I to Sir Robert Walpole, the first Prime Minister) and begins the intricate business of choosing the ministers who will help administer the country. First of all the Prime Minister will choose the most important ministers, those who go to make up the Cabinet. There are no hard and fast rules as to how many ministers there are in the Cabinet. In fact, the size of the Cabinet has been growing throughout the century, in spite of repeated declarations by Prime Ministers that they intend to reduce its size in the interests of efficiency.

One problem that faces the Prime Minister when selecting colleagues is deciding what areas of government are important enough to warrant representation in the Cabinet. Some ministers, such as the Chancellor of the Exchequer, the Foreign Secretary and the Secretary of State for Education and Science, must obviously be given Cabinet seats, but the decision is more difficult when it comes to the Secretary of State for Scotland, for example. There are those who would say that this minister could well be left out, but with 72 seats in Scotland, which could be vulnerable to Scottish Nationalists, it is a brave Prime Minister who does so. Then there are the debts that have to be paid to the different sections of the party, the left wing and the right wing, or smaller internal groups. As has been explained, both the large British political parties are to a certain extent coalitions. This means that the Prime Minister must select colleagues from all sections of the party, for if a powerful group is ignored there will inevitably be dissatisfaction. The Prime Minister must always remember that he or she is also the party leader, and ultimately this position depends on party support. So for several days the cars of potential ministers block Downing Street, while the Prime Minister examines the hand the voters have dealt, and from which the Government must be found. At the end of the period of interviewing and consulting, the Prime Minister will have a Cabinet consisting of some twenty ministers, and a further seventy to eighty junior ministers.

When they have been appointed, ministers go to Buckingham Palace, to be received by the monarch and kiss hands on appointment. The Cabinet Ministers will also be sworn in as Privy Councillors, if they are not members of the Council already (see p. 13). Most of the important ministers will be members of the Commons, but the Prime Minister must remember that there are obligations to the Lords as well, and some ministers will come from the upper house, the most important of them being the Lord Chancellor.

If the party that was in power before the election is returned to power the construction of the Government is far easier. However, the Prime Minister may use the election as an excuse to effect some changes, while it is always possible that the voters may have forced changes by failing to re-elect a former minister.

Although both the Conservative and Labour parties have 'Shadow Cabinets' (the Conservatives prefer the term 'The Leader's Committee') when in Opposition, consisting of the leading opposition spokesmen on important issues, membership of this in no way guarantees them a place in the Government if the party comes to power. The Alliance also nominates Members to speak on key issues, though as there are relatively few Alliance MPs a Member may have to take responsibility for more than one subject.

The Cabinet   The Cabinet consists of the leading ministers of the Crown, although its membership is decided by each Prime Minister individually. The Cabinet usually has around twenty members, although sometimes there may well be a smaller, unofficial group comprising an 'inner Cabinet'.

Cabinet meetings are usually held every Wednesday morning in the Cabinet Room at 10 Downing Street, although in an emergency they can be held anywhere. Discussions at these meetings are secret, and although minutes have been kept since the First World War, they are not published for thirty years. In certain cases retired senior ministers writing their memoirs have been allowed access to the Cabinet records in order to refresh their memories, and this has sometimes resulted in details of Cabinet meetings being made known before the period of thirty years has elapsed. However ex-ministers are expected to observe certain conventions. The late Richard Crossman, who served as a Labour Cabinet minister, gave detailed accounts of Cabinet meetings and also his relations with civil servants in his diaries. Although extracts from the diaries appeared in a Sunday newspaper during 1975 the question of the publication of the complete book was referred to the courts. In September 1975 permission was granted by the High Court for publication to go ahead and the first volume came out at the end of that year.

The Cabinet is the body responsible for discussing and deciding government policy and, as such, is the heart of the government system. It is presided over by the Prime Minister and it is he or she who is responsible for directing the course of meetings. Discussion is free and very often, so we are led to believe, heated, but eventually the Cabinet works out a policy that is acceptable to all. No vote is taken, but agreement is reached or assumed to be reached. Once a certain course of action has been approved by the Cabinet it becomes government policy, and all ministers accept responsibility for it, even though they may have been in bitter opposition in the Cabinet meeting. This concept of Cabinet unanimity and collective responsibility is very important, and if any minister feels that he or she cannot accept a particular decision there is no alternative but to resign.

Functions and Procedure of the House of Commons At first sight a Member of Parliament's job does not seem to be particularly arduous, and it appears that he or she earns a salary of £17,702 for very little actual work. (Members also receive an allowance of £13,211 for secretarial and research purposes.) On weekdays from Monday to Thursday the House of Commons does not meet until 2.30 p.m., and it usually adjourns at 10.30 p.m., though if necessary the House can, and does, sit through the night. On Fridays the House assembles at

10 a.m., and sits until 4.30 p.m., rising early so that MPs can visit their constituencies at the weekend.

Attendance in the Chamber, however, is only one part of parliamentary work. In addition MPs must sit on parliamentary committees, deal with the problems of constituents, keep themselves informed about affairs at home and overseas, and travel both in Britain and abroad, so conscientious Members will find that they have very little spare time.

Many MPs combine their work in Parliament with another job; for example, many barrister MPs still practise in the courts, while others, particularly on the Conservative side of the House, are engaged in business. There is considerable support for this practice, usually on the grounds that it helps Members to keep in touch with the outside world, but there are many who feel that perhaps some Members devote too much time to interests outside Parliament, and that their parliamentary work suffers.

Once an MP has been elected he or she cannot resign until the next general election. However, if for some reason the Member is unable to continue to serve he or she can apply for the post of Bailiff or Steward of the Chiltern Hundreds or the Manor of Northstead. These positions are technically offices of profit under the Crown, though they carry no actual duties, and acceptance of such office disqualifies the holder from membership of the House. Having left Parliament the ex-Member then immediately resigns the stewardship. In some cases, of course, this procedure is unnecessary because a Member has been appointed to a genuine office of profit. In December 1985 when 13 Ulster MPs registered their opposition to the Hillsborough Agreement (see p. 152) by giving up their seats at Westminster, each in turn applied for either the Chiltern Hundreds or the Manor of Northstead.

One of the first things a newly elected MP will find is that his or her 'seat' does not really exist. The Chamber of the House of Commons is too small to accommodate all the Members, and when an important debate is taking place MPs may have to find places on the stairs or in the gangways. During the Second World War the Houses of Parliament were damaged by enemy action and there were those who believed that the opportunity should be taken to rebuild the Chamber of the Commons on a more generous scale. However, Winston Churchill, who was responsible for the rebuilding, insisted that it should be restored as before, on the grounds that if the Chamber was enlarged the atmosphere of the Commons would be lost, and debates would be more difficult to follow.

The Chamber is designed with the two-party system in mind. The Government sits on one side of the House, with the Opposition on the other side, facing it. The leading ministers sit on the front bench of the Government side of the Chamber, while directly opposite them are ranged the leading spokesmen for the Opposition. Behind the 'front benchers' sit the rank and file MPs, the 'back benchers'.

Between the two rows of benches sits the Speaker, the chairman of the House, who is selected from among the Members of Parliament, and on being chosen renounces all party allegiance, to become the servant of the whole House. Because of this non-party position it is customary for the Speaker to be re-elected to subsequent Parliaments without having to contest the election. However, on a number of occasions, candidates have stood against the Speaker on the ground that the Speaker's constituents have been disenfranchised, as their MP cannot take part in parliamentary debates. Recently it has been suggested that once the Speaker has been selected by MPs he or she should be transferred to a titular constituency with no electors, but so far no move has been made to implement this suggestion. At one time the Speaker was appointed by the Crown and controlled debates on his or her royal master's behalf. Even today the Speaker is expected to show reluctance to assume office, and at the installation ceremony two Members are deputed to drag the newly appointed Speaker to the chair of the House. While acceptance of the office inevitably means the end of a political career, it has considerable compensations in terms of prestige for a Member who is prepared to accept the fact that he or she will never achieve Cabinet rank. On ceremonial occasions the Speaker represents the House of Commons and the importance of that institution is recognised by the fact that the Speaker takes precedence over all except the royal members of the House of Lords.

The Speaker is no longer a royal nominee and the Crown has lost most of its power to Parliament, but it is nevertheless still the sovereign who opens each session of Parliament with the Speech from the Throne. Each autumn the Queen drives to the Houses of Parliament and ascends the throne in the House of Lords – though technically the throne is not *in* the House of Lords. The Commons are summoned from their Chamber by the Gentleman Usher of the Black Rod. On receiving the summons the members of the House of Commons file through the Palace of Westminster, headed by the Prime Minister and the Leader of the Opposition, to take their place at the bar of the House of Lords. The contents of the Queen's Speech will hold no surprises for the Government of the day, as it is they who have been responsible for compiling it. For the other people in the Chamber, and in the country outside, the speech will be of considerable interest for it contains an outline of the legislation the Government intends to introduce during the session. After listening to the speech, the Commons return to their own Chamber for a debate on its contents, during which the opposition parties will give their reactions to the Government's proposals.

The State Opening of Parliament obviously owes much to tradition, and there are many who say that the whole procedure is out of date today; some MPs have even suggested that when Black Rod comes to call them to go to the Lords they should refuse. However the problem is that so much of the recognised procedure for conducting the business of Parliament is based on precedent and custom that to revise part of it would entail revision of the rest, and this might well upset the delicate balance between the different sections of the legislative machine. In addition to custom and precedent both Houses of Parliament have their own standing orders, and it is the duty of the Speaker to bear all these elements in mind when conducting the business of the Commons. The Speaker, or the Deputy Speaker, is responsible for supervising debates and the voting that takes place when the debate is over. They announce the result, and in the rare event of a tie have the casting vote.

From Bill to Act   There are four main classes of parliamentary Bills: Public Bills (Finance Bills), Public Bills (Non-Finance Bills), Private Members' Bills and Private Bills.

Public Bills are those which affect the whole community and can, in theory, be introduced by either the Government or the Opposition. In practice since most Public Bills involve the spending of money they are nearly always introduced by the Government. Private Members' Bills are introduced by individual MPs, while Private Bills deal with the interests of a local authority (that is, in local government), a company or an individual.

Public Bills   Before a Bill is introduced to the House, its main outline and the principles it embodies are discussed by the Cabinet and other ministers involved. Once agreement has been reached on the basic form of the Bill, it is drafted by a team of ministerial experts and lawyers. When the Bill has been prepared, the minister who is responsible for it gives notice of its intended introduction and on the appointed day the formal First Reading takes place. There is no discussion at this stage; the minister merely accepts responsibility for the Bill and the Clerk of the House reads out the title. A day is given for the Second Reading and the Bill is sent to the printers. Afterwards it is circulated to all Members so that they can study it in detail.

When the day for the Second Reading arrives the minister in charge makes a speech explaining the aims of the Bill and why it has been introduced. At the end of this speech it is proposed that 'the Bill be read a second time', and it is at this stage that the debate on the Bill begins in earnest. If the Bill is an important one it is customary for the first reply to come from the leading opposition spokesman on the matter in question, and this speech will present the party's views on the issue. The minister and the opposition front bencher speak from a position near the dispatch boxes, which are kept on the table of the Clerk of the House, but back benchers speak from where they are sitting. By convention only front benchers use notes; other Members are expected to rise from their seats and give extempore speeches. The rules of parliamentary debate are strict and are closely adhered to. Members are addressed by the Speaker and their fellow Members by the names of their constituency, the Honourable Member for —— ; members of the Privy Council are addressed as 'Right Honourable'; barristers in addition to being 'Honourable' or 'Right Honourable' are 'Learned'; while retired members of the armed forces are 'Honourable' and 'Gallant'. If a Member is referred to by name during a debate it is a rebuke from the Speaker, for a 'named' Member has offended against the rules of the House and is liable to suspension. Parliamentary procedure also distinguishes between words and phrases that are permitted and those that are not. For example, Winston Churchill once called a fellow Member a liar; on being told that 'liar' was an unparliamentary word, Churchill withdrew it and said that the Member had committed 'a terminological inexactitude', which amounts to the same thing.

The debate continues until all those who have some contribution to make have spoken, or until it is felt that proceedings must be drawn to a close because time is running out. Lack of time is one of Parliament's greatest problems, and so usually only a Bill that proposes radical changes in the law will be given sufficient time for all those interested to speak. Even so, Members are expected to keep their contributions brief, and an MP who continues for more than ten minutes will find that other Members are getting restless. Debates are usually brought to an end by the House rising at 10.30 p.m., but if necessary the House can sit after this time, even right through the night. If a Member proposes that 'the question be now put' and the proposal is accepted by at least a hundred Members the debate is brought to a close.

Sometimes it is felt necessary to speed the passage of a controversial Bill through Parliament by the use of the 'guillotine' or the 'kangaroo'. In the case of the former a timetable is worked out for the Bill and this is strictly adhered to, even though all those who want to speak on the issues it embodies have not been able to do so. The kangaroo is a procedure whereby the Speaker, or Chairman of Committees, selects only the amendments which he thinks represent important sections of opinion, so that the debate does not get bogged down over relatively unimportant matters. These methods are not used too frequently because if they were, Members might suspect that the Government was trying to limit debate on controversial topics. The Speaker can also intervene to cut short a long-winded speech or one that is irrelevant, which means that the opportunities for 'filibustering' are limited.

When the debate is ended the question is put by the Speaker. Those in favour call out 'Aye', those against 'No'. The Speaker judges the relative strength of these verbal responses and announces the result. Frequently, however, there is disagreement with the Speaker's interpretation and a Division follows. Division bells ring all over the Palace of Westminster (and in at least one public house nearby, not to mention some flats and houses in Westminster owned by MPs) and every MP who hears the bell is expected to drop what he or she is doing and rush to the Chamber to vote. Six minutes after the bells have been rung the doors of the Chamber are locked and the Members file out through the division lobbies, the 'Ayes' to the right, and the 'Noes' to the left. As the Members pass through the lobbies they are counted by tellers, who then report the numbers to the Speaker so that he can announce the result of the voting.

In theory MPs have the right to decide into which lobby they will go, but on most occasions they are expected to 'follow the party line'. If they are members of the party that is in office they are expected to vote for Government legislation, while an opposition member is expected to vote according to the directives of the party, which usually means against the Government. If Members vote in defiance of the instructions issued by the party they are likely to find themselves in serious trouble with the Whips. Each party has a Chief Whip who, with the Assistant Whips, is responsible for maintaining party discipline. (The name is derived from the 'whipper-in' in fox-hunting, whose job it is to ensure that the hounds are kept under control.) The Government Chief Whip is also the holder of a ministerial post, Parliamentary Secretary to the Treasury. The Chief Whip and Assistant Whips act as middle-men between party opinion and ministers, and play an important role in ensuring that communications are kept open between the front bench and their supporters. If controversial legislation is planned it is the duty of the Whips to make sure that the party will support the leadership and to give ample notice of any potential rebellion. The Government Chief Whip is not a member of the Cabinet but attends Cabinet meetings, so that Cabinet Ministers can be given up-to-date information about party attitudes and morale. The Whips' Office is also responsible for ensuring that there are enough MPs from the party available if a Division is called. The opposition Whips will always try to have sufficient MPs to defeat the Government, while the Whips on the Government side have to ensure that there are always enough of their Members present to prevent this happening. Whips also ensure that there is a quorum in the Chamber. If there are fewer than forty Members present a Member may challenge the quorum, the Division bells are rung, and if sufficient Members do not appear within four minutes the House is adjourned.

If a Member cannot attend a debate which is expected to end in a Division arrangements must be made to ensure that this absence will not affect the vote. This is done by finding a member of an opposing party who will also be absent and arranging a 'pair', so that they cancel each other out. On certain occasions, such as when a very important debate is taking place, the pairing system is suspended, as all parties expect their MPs to be in the Chamber, or at least within range of the Division bells. Each week every MP belonging to a major party receives a letter from the office of his party's Whips. The letter (also known as a whip) contains details of parliamentary business for the next week and informs the Member how important it is for him or her to be at Westminster. If a major debate is in the offing all parties will insist that Members cancel engagements outside London, or at least ensure that they can get back in time for the Division. So that there is no confusion over what items are considered to be of prime importance they are underlined three times, hence the expression a 'three-line whip'. A two-line whip is customary if the business is not so pressing, and in this case a Member's presence is requested unless a pair has been arranged. A one-line whip indicates that it is thought unlikely that a vote will take place.

To defy a three-line whip is tantamount to defying the party leadership. Such action will almost certainly lead to an inquiry, which could in turn lead to expulsion from the party, unless a really convincing explanation is given. It might be considered that the power exercised by the Whips is a gross interference with the freedom of the individual MPs, but the party system depends upon party unity, and should this break down organised government would soon prove impossible.

In virtually every Parliament there are MPs who leave or are expelled from their party. Sometimes the break is final. There are even cases where Members have crossed the floor of the House to join an opposition party, though on other occasions the Whip is rejected or withheld only temporarily. If a former party member has not returned to the fold by the next general election it is probable that the local constituency party will have adopted a new candidate to fight the seat. The retiring MP then has a choice of withdrawing or standing as an Independent. While, as we have seen, it is difficult for an Independent to conduct a campaign against the organisation of the major parties, it is interesting to note that in a number of cases an MP who has been rejected by the local party has nevertheless succeeded in carrying the electorate and has been returned as an Independent.

Should the Government be defeated on a Bill or if its majority is low, there will inevitably be cries of 'resign' from the opposition parties, who will claim that the Government has lost the confidence of the public.

However, a Prime Minister is not bound to resign if his or her Government is defeated on a single occasion, particularly if the defeat is the result of a snap Division, or because bad weather conditions have prevented government MPs from reaching the House. But if the Government is defeated by a large majority or if the motion on which it is defeated is one of confidence, resignation is virtually inevitable. Thus when on 28 March 1979 James Callaghan, the Labour Prime Minister, was defeated by 311 votes to 310 on the motion that 'This House has no confidence in Her Majesty's Government' he was faced with two options. He could either have resigned and advised the Queen to ask the Leader of the Opposition (Margaret Thatcher) to form a Government from among the members of the Conservative Party, or sought a dissolution of Parliament, to be followed by a general election. He decided to opt for a dissolution, and in the ensuing general election was defeated – the Conservatives winning 339 seats to Labour's 268. Callaghan's defeat on a no confidence motion was the first by a Government since 1924 when his Labour predecessor, Ramsay Mac-Donald suffered the same fate.

In practice, a Government with a comfortable majority can be virtually certain of getting its Bills passed, particularly if they are dealing with important issues. The Thatcher Government which succeeded Callaghan's certainly had no problems in introducing a large number of controversial measures into the House and getting the necessary legislation passed. They did, however, encounter a certain amount of opposition to some measures from the House of Lords (in spite of that Chamber's built-in Conservative majority) and were forced to back down on a number of issues. Mrs Thatcher was re-elected in 1983 with an even larger majority than she enjoyed in 1979 but once again the Government was to find that the House of Lords was not to be taken for granted. Their Lordships blocked a number of Bills – including some of the legislation relating to the abolition of the Greater London Council (see p. 51) although in this case the legislation came back to the Commons for re-endorsement (see p. 44).

After the Second Reading, the Bill moves to the Committee Stage, where it is taken apart and discussed in detail, clause by clause. Important Bills, including all Finance Bills, are considered by a Committee of the Whole House. When this occurs the mace, the symbol of the Speaker's authority, is placed below the Clerk's table, and the Speaker vacates the chair, to be replaced by a chairman who conducts the ensuing discussion in a more informal manner than when the House is debating a motion. The Committee ends when the motion 'That the chairman do report progress and ask leave to sit again' has been passed. The mace is then restored to its usual position and the Speaker resumes the chair. Less important Bills are dealt with by the five or six Standing Committees. These committees consist of between twenty and fifty MPs selected from all parties, in the ratio in which their parties are represented in the Commons. Committees usually sit in the morning, in special rooms in the Palace of Westminster, and tend to be very time-consuming. The Committee reports back to the House after it has considered the Bill, and it is at this stage that the amendments proposed by the Committee are either accepted or rejected by the proposer, while further amendments can also be put forward. Not infrequently, a Bill is referred back to the Committee for further discussion. (Standing Committees must not be confused with Select Committees, which are appointed to inquire into and report to the House on special matters. Select Committees may be appointed for a particular purpose, or they may be appointed at the beginning of a session in order that they are in being to consider any issues that might arise during the session. Sessional committees include the Select Committee on Estimates and the Committee of Privileges.)

After the Committee Stage the Bill is given a Third Reading, and if it is passed it goes to the House of Lords. Here it goes through the same stages as it did in the Commons, though if the Lords propose amendments that alter the nature of the Bill, it must be returned to the Commons for further discussion. The Lords may not reject a Finance Bill, nor can they delay any other Bill for more than one session. The implications of this are discussed in the section on the House of Lords (p. 44). If a Bill has been initiated in the House of Lords it must then go to the House of Commons for discussion.

Once a Bill has been passed by the Lords it is given the Royal Assent. This assent is usually given in Letters Patent and then announced by the Speakers of both Houses. Once this has been done the Bill becomes an Act. Although in theory the sovereign can refuse to give consent to a Bill, in practice this right has not been exercised since the early eighteenth century, during the reign of Queen Anne.

Private Bills Private Bills are usually promoted by local authorities, though personal Private Bills can be put forward by any citizen or group of citizens. However, largely due to the expense of briefing a lawyer to defend the Bill in Committee and the cost of getting a Bill drawn up in the first place, personal Private Bills are rare today. Private Bills introduced by local authorities usually deal with land purchase, and often concern the taking over of graveyards or obtaining the necessary powers for development.

Private Members' Bills are Bills introduced by individual Members of Parliament. At the beginning of each session a ballot is held, and MPs who come high enough in this are permitted to introduce a Bill on a matter that is of particular interest to them. A number of Fridays are set aside for the discussion of Private Members' Bills, but only those who come reasonably high in the ballot will stand much chance of getting their Bill debated. Some of these Fridays are reserved for the First Reading of Private Members' Bills and the remainder for later stages, so even if a Member gets his Bill through the First Reading it may get no further.

Apart from time there are other factors that work against Private Members' Bills. In the first place the Bill must be drawn up, a difficult task requiring expert advice, because a badly worded Bill will be torn to pieces by critics. Even when a Member has a Bill, and parliamentary time to introduce it, the troubles of the would-be legislator are not over. One of the rocks on which many Private Members' Bills founder is the 'counting out' of the House, for there are no party Whips to ensure that there is a quorum. This is a common way for opponents of a Bill to stop its progress, for attendances on Fridays are often very poor. Another problem may be that instead of there being too few MPs interested in the Bill, there are too many. As we have seen there are relatively few days available for the discussion of Private Members's Bills, and if the opponents of a controversial Bill can make the debate stretch out, the end of the session may be reached before the Bill has been passed. A Bill that has not completed its passage through Parliament in one session must be reintroduced and the whole process begun all over again. The only way to get over this difficulty is for the Government to give parliamentary time to enable a Bill to be discussed. Private Members' Bills dealing with controversial matters that the Government of the day is, for one reason or another, unwilling to introduce, but to which it is broadly speaking sympathetic, may therefore be debated and passed outside the time reserved for Private Members' Bills.

If Members are unlucky in the ballot for Private Members' Bills they still have an opportunity to introduce a Bill under the 'ten-minute rule'. Any Tuesday or Wednesday, at the end of Question Time, an MP may propose a Bill and speak in favour of it for ten minutes. After this any other Member can speak against his Bill for the same amount of time. The Speaker then 'puts the question', and if the House accepts it this First Reading is considered complete. The problem now faced by the proposer is to find the time for the next stages of the Bill. If it can be classified as 'unfinished business' it can be dealt with during the Debate on the Adjournment, provided that no other Member objects, for the opposition of a single MP is enough to stop it on this occasion. The main purpose of the adjournment debate is to allow Members to raise important business. At 10.30 p.m. the House completes the business it has been discussing, and the motion 'That this House do now adjourn' is proposed, which leads to a further debate on some question of

Government policy, or any other matter not requiring legislation. Other motions to adjourn may be on matters of great public import- ance, which cannot be debated at any other time. A member of the Government can put forward such a motion immediately after Question Time, before any other item on the Order Paper (that is, the order of business for the day) is taken. Any other Member may also propose an emergency motion at the same time, but if this motion is to be accepted it must be supported by at least forty other Members. If the support required is obtained the motion is debated at 7 p.m., and takes precedence over all other business. An emergency debate can, if necessary, continue after the normal time for the adjournment of the House at 10.30 p.m.; however such debates only take place if the Speaker is convinced that a case for urgency has been made.

Question Time gives the individual MP another opportunity to have an influence on the conduct of the Government. Question Time takes place at about 2.40 p.m. every day immediately after Private Business, and lasts for about an hour. Two days' notice of questions must be given, and most questions are answered in writing. If they wish, however, Members can insist that the minister to whom the question is put answers it orally in the House of Commons. When the question has been answered the Speaker allows supplementary questions, and often a skilled questioner will reserve the full force of the question for the supplementary, thus hoping to catch the minister off-guard. If the Member is still unsatisfied after pursuing the matter through a supplementary, notice can be given that it will be raised again on the adjournment.

Parliamentary Questions are of considerable importance in the British system of government, because they give individual Members a chance to keep a check on the executive. All ministers, from the Prime Minister downwards, are liable to be questioned, and on some occasions an apparently harmless question has revealed a highly unsatisfactory state of affairs. More than once a minister has had to resign as a result of information that was first brought to light by a Parliamentary Question. Not all questions are of such a dramatic nature, however, and many are the result of a constituent complaining of an injustice to the local MP, who then follows the matter up with a question to the minister concerned.

All the business of the House as outlined above takes place in public, except on rare occasions when matters of national security are discussed. A record is kept of all debates and questions and these are printed in the Official Report, known to all as Hansard, after the printer who was appointed to do the job in 1812.

Since June 1975 radio transmissions have taken place from both the House of Commons and the House of Lords – but the Commons have refused to allow television cameras into their chamber. In 1983 the Lords agreed to permit the televising of debates for an experimental period and in 1985, and again in 1986, this was extended. The same year the Commons voted once again against televising the proceedings of their House which means that even for important debates the general public is dependent on the radio transmission and an artist's sketch of the scene within the House of Commons which is rarely very helpful in providing any sense of the reality of the debate.

THE HOUSE OF LORDS

The upper chamber of Parliament is known as the House of Lords and its membership is made up of the Lords Temporal, that is, hereditary peers and life peers; and the Lords Spiritual, the bishops of the Church of England.

The largest group are the hereditary peers, that is, men (and a few women who are peeresses in their own right) who possess hereditary titles. They fall into several different categories. In the first place there are the royal Dukes, members of the royal family who have seats in the Lords, but who in fact rarely participate in debates. Next come the non-royal Dukes, the senior of whom is the Duke of Norfolk, hereditary Earl Marshal of England, whose title dates from 1483. Dukes are followed by Marquesses, who are comparatively rare, and then come Earls, Viscounts and Barons. All these titles pass to the next male in line on the death of the holder; if there is no heir the title dies out. Although the aristocracy has existed since Norman times few of the present titles are very ancient, virtually all of them being post-1600. At one time kings found titles a convenient way to reward favourites, while at some periods of history titles have been sold openly, or with very little attempt at concealment. The early Stuarts, for example, used the sale of titles to bolster their revenues when Parliament was reluctant to grant them money.

At the present time there are just over 1,000 people who have the right to sit in the House of Lords (about 200 of these are life peers, 26 are bishops and archbishops of the Church of England and the rest are hereditary peers), though not all of them choose to do so. In addition to the royal Dukes a number of other peers apply for, and are granted, leave of absence. There are probably fewer than 200 peers who take a regular part in debates, although others will attend if they are particularly interested in the subject that is under discussion. The creation of peers is the prerogative of the sovereign, but in practice it is the Prime Minister who decides whether new peers are to be created, and who they should be.

Life peerages were introduced in 1958. As the name suggests life peers hold their titles for the duration of their lives and the title becomes redundant on death. Although it is the Prime Minister who draws up the lists of new peers it should not be thought that he or she recommends only members of his or her own party to the monarch. When new peers are created, for example in the Dissolution (of Parliament) Honours or in the New Year Honours, the other party leaders are asked to make their recommendations. Nevertheless, party politics plays an important part in the Lords and one of the problems faced by a Labour administration is that there is a massive Conservative majority in the upper house.

Churchmen have sat in the Lords since its earliest days, and at one time the abbots from the leading monasteries attended as well as the bishops. Today the Lords Spiritual consist of twenty-six Anglican bishops: the Archbishops of Canterbury and York, the Bishops of London, Winchester and Durham, and twenty-one other bishops in order of seniority. The bishops sit as representatives of the Established Church, the Church of England. There is no provision for other churchmen to sit in the Lords, though a prominent Methodist minister was made a life peer some years ago. It has been suggested that a similar honour should be bestowed upon the Roman Catholic Archbishop of Westminster, but as yet the proposal has not been put into effect.

The ten law lords, who comprise the supreme judiciary of Great Britain, sit in the House by virtue of being Lords of Appeal in Ordinary. They are life peers and when they retire as law lords they retain their seats. Their functions are dealt with in Chapter 4.

Unlike MPs, members of the House of Lords are not paid a salary, although they can claim expenses for each day they attend debates. The House of Lords sits shorter hours than does the Commons, and does not sit on Fridays.

The House of Lords is presided over by the Lord Chancellor, who sits on the Woolsack (a large cushion stuffed with wool from Britain and the Commonwealth; wool was Britain's most important export in the

Middle Ages) and fulfils the same functions as the Speaker in the House of Commons. However, unlike the Speaker, the Lord Chancellor is an active politician, appointed by the Prime Minister and with a seat in the Cabinet. The Lord Chancellor is also head of the legal profession and has important functions associated with this position, as we shall see when we look at the legal system (see Chapter 4). When the Lord Chancellor wishes to participate in a debate the Woolsack is vacated, and another member of the House, usually the Chairman of Committees, takes over the responsibility of presiding over the House.

Functions of the House of Lords   The House of Lords has two main functions: it is the second chamber of Parliament with the right to discuss legislation; and it is also the highest court in the land.

Until the beginning of the twentieth century the House of Lords was theoretically equal in status to the House of Commons, though in fact it was clear that all major decisions were made by the lower house. The last Prime Minister to sit in the Lords was Lord Salisbury, who resigned in 1902.

In 1911 the Parliament Act was passed which placed limitations on the power of the Lords. The Act said that the Lords could not in future reject a Bill that had been passed by the Commons, although they could delay it for two years. Money Bills had to be passed within a month of their coming from the Commons. (The Act also contained some clauses not directly related to the issue of the Lords, including providing a salary for MPs and making a reduction in the life of Parliament from seven to five years.)

However, the 1911 Act did not seem to have the desired effect as the Lords still obstructed Bills, and even today when the delaying power of the Lords is only a year (since 1947) some Bills are halted by the upper house simply because the Commons does not have the time to discuss them again. (A Bill rejected by the Lords must go all the way through the Commons again, even though it has already been passed there once.) Of course, the Government will find time for a Bill that it considers important, but some measures are in effect killed by the Lords. Private Members' Bills in particular often run into difficulty in the upper house. Few peers would want to risk a head-on collision with the Commons, but they have a number of ways in which they can delay government business if they wish – ways that are more subtle than outright rejection. In 1967 proposals were made to reduce the power of the Lords, and in 1969 a proposition was debated that would have

44

restricted the voting rights of hereditary peers. However, when it became obvious that to get the proposed Bill through would entail a major parliamentary battle, lasting many months, the plans were dropped. We have also seen (p. 38) that even a Conservative Prime Minister is not able to take the Lords for granted.

So the House of Lords survives, and there are many who would support its existence. It is often claimed that the Lords provides a useful second opinion on legislation; amendments can be suggested and new opinions expressed. Another argument in favour of the Lords is that, as they have more time than the Commons, they can discuss a Bill in far greater detail. It is also frequently suggested that this discussion can be freer than it is in the Commons, because the Lords do not have constituencies to worry about, or electors to offend, and so they can speak more freely on controversial issues. This is a rather peculiar argument, for it draws attention to the fact that the Lords represent nobody but themselves. It also raises the whole question of whether Parliament should take public opinion into account, and whether Parliament is, or should be, responsible to the people – a question of vital importance to a democracy (see also p. 6).

The introduction of life peers in 1958 produced another argument in favour of the retention of the House of Lords. It was suggested that the Lords might become a forum of experts, and that distinguished people who did not have the time or inclination to fight an election or nurse a constituency could still be recruited to give the country the benefit of their experience. This is an interesting argument in theory, but it is not borne out in practice. Although it is true that some eminent doctors, scientists and academics have become life peers, most have been chosen from the ranks, or at least the fringes, of the political parties, Nor does this argument explain why hereditary peers should retain the right to sit in the House of Lords.

As far as the Prime Minister is concerned the House of Lords certainly has its uses. It can be used as a dumping ground for Members of Parliament who have safe seats but little political value. The ennoblement of such a person vacates the seat, which then can be allocated to a potential minister. The Lords can also be used by the Prime Minister to bring new blood into the Government when a by-election might prove embarrassing. The Prime Minister can make the candidate for the position a life peer, thus providing a seat in the House of Lords.

An argument frequently put forward in favour of the retention of the

House of Lords is that the Lords safeguards the constitution. According to this argument it is claimed that the Commons could, if they were so inclined, change the whole British system of government in an afternoon by a single majority vote. This argument means, of course, that the Lords, who as we have seen represent only themselves, exist to protect the British people against their elected representatives. Should the Lords be abolished it might be thought necessary to introduce safeguards into the system to limit the power of the Commons, but these could probably be arranged without much difficulty. In some countries, for instance, constitutional changes require the approval of the people in the form of a referendum, while in others such legislation can only be passed if the representative chamber approves the measures by a large enough majority, usually in the order of two-thirds. There seems no reason why similar procedures could not be adopted in the United Kingdom, particularly as the referendum device has already been used in relation to Common Market membership.

Until recently, peers who inherited titles were forced to accept them whether they wanted to or not. Thus politicians who were making a name for themselves in the House of Commons might suddenly find that they were elevated to the House of Lords, where they would get prestige and the guarantee of a seat in one of the legislative chambers, but would stand little chance of gaining the highest political office. A number of people who found themselves in this situation had complained bitterly about it, but had resigned themselves to what they considered to be the inevitable. However, in the early 1960s Mr Anthony Wedgwood Benn, a prominent Labour MP, found himself transformed overnight into Viscount Stansgate when his father died. In spite of his objections he was told that he had no option but to give up his parliamentary seat in Bristol and take his place in the House of Lords. He accordingly vacated his seat, but at the ensuing by-election he stood as a candidate and was returned with a comfortable majority. He then tried to take his seat in the Commons, but was refused admittance to the Chamber. An electoral court subsequently awarded the seat to the Conservative who had been runner-up. Wedgwood Benn's campaign, however, had aroused considerable interest and sympathy, and in 1963 the Peerage Act was passed. Under the terms of this Act a person who inherits a peerage is permitted to disclaim it for his lifetime, and on his death it passes to the next in line. The first person to take advantage of the Act was, of course, Lord Stansgate who speedily returned to the Commons, and in due course became a Cabinet Minister.

Following the defeat of the Labour Party at the 1979 election, Tony Benn (as he has chosen to call himself), a Cabinet Minister in the outgoing government, has concentrated on building himself a power base on the left wing of the Labour Party. In 1981 he stood as a candidate in the election for deputy leader of the party. He was defeated, but it was interesting to note that in the election he secured considerable support from the constituency parties and to a lesser extent from the trade unions – the bulk of the opposition came from Labour MPs.

Shortly after the Peerage Act was passed a prominent Conservative, Viscount Hailsham, renounced his title in the hope of becoming leader of the Conservative Party and Prime Minister on the resignation of Mr Macmillan. As Quintin Hogg he was elected MP for Marylebone, but in the event the leadership went to another member of the Lords, the Earl of Home, who became Prime Minister as Sir Alec Douglas-Home. Subsequently both these gentlemen have returned to the Lords as life peers, as Lord Hailsham of St Marylebone and Lord Home of the Hirsel. In 1979 Lord Hailsham was appointed Lord Chancellor, a post he retained when Mrs Thatcher was returned to power in 1983.

Ministries

In recent years a number of 'super-ministries' have been established, some of which incorporate smaller ministries which at one time had a separate existence. For example, the Department of the Environment includes ministries responsible for local government and housing. Each of the 'super-ministries' is headed by a Secretary of State, who is assisted by a number of junior ministers, ministers of state and under-secretaries of state.

Each ministry is staffed by civil servants under a permanent secretary. The civil servants are responsible for advising their ministers and for putting the decisions taken by the politicians in Parliament into effect. In theory civil servants do not take decisions themselves, but in practice they wield considerable power. Much of their power comes from the fact that while the minister holds the job for a relatively short period of time, the civil servant is a permanent official who over the years can acquire considerable expertise in a particular field. Many have expressed considerable misgivings about the growth in the influence of Whitehall (the area of London where most of the important ministries are found), and one of the tasks of the Fulton Committee which reported in 1968 was to see whether far-reaching reforms were required. A number of Fulton's recommendations were put into effect, although there seems little evidence that far-reaching changes have taken place regarding either recruitment or patterns of service. In 1979 the Thatcher government, like others before it, announced that it intended to carry out a radical review of the entire civil service with the aim of reducing the number of positions in government service. This was coupled with the intention of the government to 'privatise' many of the state-owned service and manufacturing industries (see also p. 106).

Royal Commissions

The reader will find reference to a number of Royal Commissions in this book. Royal Commissions are committees set up by the Government to investigate and make recommendations on various matters. They invite evidence from interested individuals and bodies; this is sifted and then examined and a report is issued. The Government is not bound to accept the advice of a Royal Commission.

3

Local Government

In recent years a great deal of attention has been paid to the question of local government reform. No less than three Royal Commissions, appointed to inquire into the problems of local government in different areas of the country, presented their reports during the 1960s: the Royal Commission on Local Government in London in 1960; the Royal Commission on Local Government in England and the Royal Commission on Local Government in Scotland in 1969. A fourth Royal Commission reported in October 1973. This was the Kilbrandon Commission on the Constitution, which among other things recommended the setting up of assemblies with limited powers for Scotland and Wales. It also suggested that some form of regional self-government should be established within England, although these recommendations have not been acted upon. Nor have the suggestions regarding devolution for Scotland and Wales been put into effect, as it was decided that the support for this, as manifested in the devolution referendums, was far from universal. However, following the decision not to proceed, many of those living in Scotland and Wales have continued to press for more local control of their destinies.

The traditional units of English local government were the parish, the borough and the county. As is the case with so many other British institutions, they originally fulfilled functions far different from those that they were later called upon to undertake. The parish was in its early days an ecclesiastical unit, the centre of which was the parish church. During the sixteenth and seventeenth centuries it acquired civil functions, such as the maintenance of highways and care of the poor. Borough status was granted by the Crown. Apart from the prestige of receiving a charter, the honour was a coveted one because it gave towns a certain amount of independence. Boroughs had their own courts, and they could also hold markets and send representatives to Parliament. The county was originally the territory granted to an earl by the king in return for feudal service. In spite of the fact that a feudal lord's fief is not necessarily the most suitable basis for modern administrative purposes, the basic outline of the English counties, particularly in the south of the country, has varied little from the Middle Ages.

In 1835 boroughs became the first local government units to acquire some degree of democracy. The Municipal Corporations Act provided for a system of local councillors elected by ratepayers, while a quarter of the council were 'aldermen', elected by the councillors. The Local Government Act of 1888 introduced a system of county councils, elected by ratepayer franchise as in the boroughs. The Act also clarified the relationship between local and national government and between county and borough councils. Although the idea of an elected county council was new, the areas of the counties remained much the same as they had been prior to 1888, the only major change being that some of the larger counties were subdivided. Thus shortly after the Act was passed sixty-two county councils had been formed from the fifty-two geographical counties.

The structure of local government established in the nineteenth century remained in force until well into the twentieth. In 1966, however, a Royal Commission on Local Government was appointed and its report was published in 1969. In essence it proposed a sweeping away of the old local authorities, replacing them with a system of fifty-eight unitary and three metropolitan authorities. The Maud Report, as it was called after its chairman Lord Redcliffe-Maud, was much discussed at national and local level. In 1970 the Labour Government produced a White Paper in which it accepted the proposals of the Commission, although with a number of modifications. But before the Government could make these reforms law, Labour was defeated at the general election of July 1970. The incoming Conservatives produced their revised plans for the reform of local government in February 1971, and in 1972 the Local Government Reorganisation Act established a new pattern of local authorities which came into effect on 1 April 1974.

The local authorities set up in 1974 included the Greater London Council (responsible for local government in the capital), 6 metropolitan counties, made up of the largest conurbations, and 30 non-metropolitan counties. Both the metropolitan and non-metropolitan councils were subdivided into districts, of which 36 were in metropolitan councils and 296 in non-metropolitan councils. Although the legislation setting up the new system of local government was introduced by the Conservatives, their successors a decade later felt that further reform was necessary. They argued that the metropolitan councils were too large and unwieldy to operate efficiently and they announced that they were proposing to abolish the councils and redistribute power to the constituent districts. In spite of bitter opposition from the councils, who argued that the legislation was inspired by party rather than financial considerations – the majority of councils were Labour-controlled – and some unexpected resistance from the Lords (see page 38) the government prevailed, and in 1986 the metropolitan councils and the Greater London Council disappeared.

County councils are responsible for planning, roads, public transport, waste disposal, consumer protection and police and fire services. County councils and district authorities are responsible for education, youth employment, personal social services, libraries, housing and local planning. Museums and art galleries, conservation areas, airports and the acquisition and disposal of land for planning purposes are subject to control by both district and county authorities. In the old metropolitan areas control of the police, fire service and public transport is vested in joint boards comprised of councillors nominated by district councils.

Since 1974 Scotland has been divided into 9 regions for local government purposes, with a second tier of 53 districts – there are also local authorities with responsibility for the island communities of Orkney, Shetland and the Western Isles. Local government in Wales is in the hands of 8 counties, instead of 13 that existed prior to local government reform. Northern Ireland has 26 district councils, while services such as education, housing, education and planning are administered centrally from Belfast, the capital of the province.

Local councils consist of a number of elected councillors presided over by a chairman. Some districts have the ancient rank of borough, now purely a ceremonial title, and some are known as cities. In boroughs the chairman is granted the courtesy title of Mayor while in certain large or ancient cities he is the Lord Mayor (in Scottish burghs the titles are Provost and Lord Provost). Councillors hold office for four years; in counties they stand for electoral divisions, in districts for wards.

Expenditure by local authorities is financed from the following sources: grants from central government, local rates and rents from council houses and flats, dividends and interest. The size of the government grant depends on the size of the council and the number of people it must provide for. Another factor that is taken into account is the age composition of the population, particularly the numbers of old and young people, as education and old people's homes are provided by local authorities.

Rates are a form of tax levied on occupants of non-agricultural land and buildings. The amount each ratepayer contributes is calculated by multiplying the rateable value of his or her property (that is, roughly the amount the property would bring in if it was to be rented out) by the rate poundage (a percentage fixed by the authority according to its anticipated needs). Rates are paid by the head of the household, and although other people living in the house may contribute to the sum required there is no obligation for them to do so. This means that if a man lives by himself in a house his rate bill may well be the same as that of his next-door neighbour who is married and has three grown-up children living with him. (Even so, lodgers who do not pay rates are still entitled to vote in local elections.)

The rate system has come under considerable attack in recent years and many have argued in favour of a form of local income or 'poll tax' – including many politicians. However, although politicians out of office seem to agree that the existing system is unsatisfactory, when they achieve power the reform of the rates system becomes a low priority. In 1986, partly due to a tension that had been building up for some time between local and national government over large-scale rate increases, the Government issued a discussion document on the reform of local government finance. It is too early, however, to say whether any major changes in the system will be introduced. One bone of contention that is unlikely to go away is the dispute between local authorities and central government over the issue of who should pay for what. The Conservative government, with its policy of reducing government expenditure, has refused to increase the amount of 'rate support grant' paid to local authorities and, in some cases, has taken action against councils who it considers to have been overspending.

4

The Legal System

The legal system of England and Wales has evolved over a considerable period of time. Its origins can be traced back to before the Norman Conquest of 1066. Whereas in many countries there is a criminal and civil code, in England and Wales the two main elements of law are common law, which is largely dependent on precedent, and statute law, which consists of Acts of Parliament (though the division between criminal and civil law is fully recognised). Scottish law differs from that of England and Wales in a number of important respects, and the procedure and officials of the Scottish courts are peculiar to that country.

Courts in England and Wales

CRIMINAL COURTS
Since the Courts Act of 1971 came into force at the beginning of 1972, there have been two levels of criminal courts in England and Wales. Magistrates' courts deal with the great majority of criminal cases, while more serious offences are dealt with by the Crown courts, which replaced the Assizes and Quarter Sessions.

Magistrates' Courts Magistrates' courts are (except in London and a few large towns) presided over by lay Justices of the Peace (JPs), who sit on the bench part-time, and receive no salary for their services. The jurisdiction of the magistrates' courts is local, counties being divided into petty sessional divisions, while each town of any size has its own court. The court has three main functions. First, it hears and deter-mines charges against people accused of summary offences, that is offences that are not serious enough to go before higher courts. The magistrates' courts may also try certain indictable offences, offences of a more serious nature, with the agreement of the accused. Normally indictable offences are tried by a court with a jury, but in some cases the accused person may prefer to have the case dealt with by the two to seven magistrates sitting on the bench in the lower court. This may be to the advantage of the accused if he or she is found guilty, as the sentences imposed by a magistrates' court are less than those of the higher court. On the other hand, there is a chance that a jury will take a more sympathetic view of the offence than the magistrates, and decline to convict. About 98 per cent of all criminal cases are disposed of in the magistrates' courts.

The second function of the magistrates' court is to conduct a preliminary hearing, to decide whether there is sufficient evidence to commit the accused for trial in a higher court. Thirdly the magistrates hear cases involving children. Juvenile courts hear cases in which children under 14 are brought before the court as being in need of care and protection. They also administer justice in criminal proceedings brought against young people between the ages of 14 and 17.

In addition to these judicial functions, the magistrates act as licensing authorities for public houses, restaurants, betting shops and other public places.

There are about 25,000 lay magistrates, sitting in nearly 700 different centres. As the magistrates rarely have any formal legal education there are frequently considerable discrepancies between sentencing policy in different parts of the country. Some studies have shown that while the magistrates in one court will be particularly hard on one offence, magistrates in another place will adopt a far more liberal attitude. Factors such as this have led many people to criticise the system, and to suggest that magistrates' courts should be replaced by courts presided over by professional lawyers. However, the lay Justice of the Peace has a history dating back to the fourteenth century, and there are many, including most magistrates, who would be loath to see the office disappear.

In spite of the fact that magistrates are unpaid and only receive small allowances, there is no shortage of people who would like to sit on the bench. Appointments are made by the Lord Chancellor on the recommendation of a local committee for each area, and in theory anyone without a criminal record can become a JP. In practice, most magistrates tend to be middle-class people, and the great majority of them are over 50 years old. One is far more likely to find a retired doctor or army officer presiding over a magistrates' court than a plumber or engine driver, retired or still at work. Nor has the old role of the Justice of the Peace as the country gentleman been entirely forgotten and many magistrates, particularly in country areas, are appointed on what appears to be an almost hereditary basis. A large number of JPs are people who are, or have been, prominent in local government or 'public life', and appointment to the bench is often regarded as a recognition of public service, as it confers considerable social prestige.

Since 1966 it has been compulsory for newly appointed justices to participate in training courses, and to attend court as observers before actually taking their seats on the bench. Even so the magistrate still relies a great deal on the guidance of the magistrates' clerk, who is a lawyer appointed as legal adviser to the bench, and in all except the smallest courts is a full-time official.

Stipendiary Magistrates   In London and a few of the larger provincial cities there are full-time stipendiary magistrates (as well as JPs) who sit alone. The stipendiary magistrates – there are thirty-seven in London and a further eleven in other cities – are trained lawyers and, unlike their lay counterparts, they receive a salary. Suggestions have been made that the use of stipendiary magistrates should be extended, but the proposal has been resisted by the legal profession who claim that there are not enough lawyers, and the lay magistrates who are reluctant to see their powers reduced.

Crown Courts   In 1966 the Government established a Royal Commission to prepare a report on Assizes and Quarter Sessions, under Lord Beeching. In 1969 the report was published and as a result the Courts Act was passed in 1971. By this Act the ancient courts of Assize and Quarter Sessions, which had their origins in the thirteenth century, were abolished, and in their place Crown courts were set up.

Under the old system Quarter Sessions were held in each of the counties of England and Wales, in ninety-three boroughs and Greater London, and the City of London. In the counties cases were heard before magistrates who sat under a legally qualified chairman. In the boroughs, with their own Quarter Sessions, the proceedings were presided over by a Recorder who was responsible for passing sentence, although guilt or innocence was decided by a jury of twelve. Juries were also found in the courts of Assize, which were branches of the High Court, presided over by a High Court judge. The courts of

Assize were held in assize towns (usually the county town of each county) and in other large towns or cities. For the purpose of the assize the country was divided into seven 'circuits'. The judge allocated to the circuit visited each assize town in turn; each town was visited at least once, the larger ones twice. The Assize court for Greater London was the Central Criminal Court, sitting at the Old Bailey, which was in continuous session.

The system of Crown courts retains the circuits, but these have been reduced from seven to six. The circuits and their administrative centres are: south-eastern (London), midland and Oxford (Birmingham), north-eastern (Leeds), Wales and Chester (Cardiff), western (Bristol) and northern (Manchester). The Crown courts are served by a bench of circuit judges and also by judges of the High Court. According to the Act of 1971, towns with Crown courts are divided up into 'first-tier', 'second-tier' and 'third-tier' centres. In first-tier centres both High Court and circuit judges deal with criminal cases and the High Court judges also hear civil cases. In second-tier centres the High Court and circuit judges only deal with criminal cases, while in third-tier centres there are only circuit judges trying criminal cases.

The bench of circuit judges introduced by the Courts Act is made up from the county court bench, the full-time judges sitting in criminal courts, such as the Old Bailey, and a number of new appointments. The qualification for becoming a circuit judge is to have been a barrister (see p. 61) for ten years, or a Recorder (a part-time judge) for at least five.

Like the Assize courts, Crown courts have a jury of twelve and try indictable, that is the more serious, criminal offences. They also act as appeal courts for people convicted of an offence in the magistrates' court. A person found guilty in a magistrates' court can plead against either conviction or sentence, although if he has pleaded guilty in the lower court he may only appeal against sentence. Appeals from the crown courts go to the Criminal Division of the Court of Appeal, and in some cases from there to the House of Lords (see p. 44).

Court Procedure   Although it is possible for any private citizen to institute criminal proceedings, in practice prosecutions are usually initiated by the police. In serious or contentious cases details are sent to the Director of Public Prosecutions, and it is he who decides whether the case should be proceeded with or not.

Arrests are usually made by police officers – although in law any citizen is empowered to make an arrest – with or without a warrant.

Under the Police and Criminal Evidence Act which came into force in January 1986 a person can be detained in custody without charge for up to ninety-six hours. Once charged, a defendant can be freed on bail, although if the police consider that he or she might disappear they are entitled to object to bail, and ask that the defendant be kept in custody. The decision, however, is left to the magistrate. If a person is freed on bail, securities must be given, either by the accused or by someone acting for him or her. In serious cases the accused is usually remanded until the case against him or her has been prepared. If a person who is detained considers that this detention is unlawful he or she can apply for a writ of *habeas corpus* which requires that cause for the detention is shown before the courts.

English criminal law assumes that a person is innocent until proved guilty. It is the responsibility of the prosecution to show beyond any reasonable doubt that the defendant has committed the offence of which he or she is accused. If this cannot be done a verdict of not guilty must be returned. Everyone accused of an offence has the right to employ a legal adviser to present their case, and if they cannot afford to do so they can be provided with legal aid at public expense. All criminal trials, with a few exceptions, such as those involving official secrets, are heard in open court, and the trial is conducted according to strict rules of procedure. All evidence must be given in the presence of the accused, and the defendant, or his or her counsel, has the right to question all the witnesses. The prosecution may also question the defence witnesses, but they cannot cross-question the accused, unless he or she decides to go into the witness-box.

As the terms 'prosecution' and 'defence' suggest, an English trial is a contest, in which both sides try to convince the jury that the case which they are presenting is the truth. The judge acts as referee in this contest, and when one side thinks that its opponents are breaking the rules it can appeal to the judge for a ruling. The judge's powers of interference are limited, and he or she may only intervene in order to check an over-zealous barrister, to advise on a point of law, or to clarify an obscure point. Should the judge interfere too actively, or show partiality to one side or the other, this may form the basis of an appeal in a higher court.

After the prosecution and defence have concluded their cases, and both sides have presented their final speeches, it is the judge's duty to sum up. In the summing-up speech the judge is expected to outline the case and explain the legal issues involved to the jury. Once the judge has summed up the jury consider their verdict, and in serious cases this can take quite a long time. Should it become apparent that the jury cannot decide on a verdict they will be discharged and a new jury will be selected to hear the trial all over again. However in the vast majority of cases the jury is able to come to a decision. Until 1967 the verdict of the jury had to be unanimous, but since then majority decisions are acceptable, providing that there are not more than two dissentients. If a verdict of not guilty is arrived at, the accused is freed at once. If he or she is found guilty it is the judge's responsibility to pronounce sentence. This may be done at once, or the judge may in certain circumstances adjourn the court so that he or she has time to consider what penalty should be imposed. Some judges use the opportunity of passing sentence to deliver a few well-chosen words about the defendant and the crime he or she has committed, or on occasion about society in general.

Criminal Appeal　A person convicted in a magistrates' court can appeal against conviction or sentence to the Crown court. There is also an appeal in some cases to the High Court. Appeals from the Crown courts against conviction or sentence are made to the Court of Appeal (Criminal Division). An appeal against conviction is brought on a point of law – if, for example, it is felt that the judge at the trial has misinterpreted a legal point – or on a question of fact. Appeals against sentence depend on whether the sentence was at the discretion of the judge. The Court of Appeal (Criminal Division) consists of three judges, either Lords Justices of Appeal or judges of the High Court. They are usually presided over by the Lord Chief Justice or a Justice of Appeal. Appeal from the Court of Appeal to the House of Lords is permitted if it is felt that a point of law of general public importance is involved. A prosecutor or defendant can also appeal to the Lords over a decision of the High Court in a criminal case.

CIVIL COURTS
Civil actions are tried before county courts, before High Court judges sitting in Crown courts, or in the High Court itself. Until they were abolished Assize courts heard civil actions after all the criminal cases on the list had been disposed of. Magistrates' courts also have some limited civil jurisdiction. They can deal with matrimonial proceedings for separation (but not divorce), maintenance orders, adoptions and guardianship.

The county courts were established in 1846 to handle civil cases. At the present time their jurisdiction is limited to actions founded on contract and tort (a private or civil wrong) up to a specified limit and certain actions relating to the recovery of land. Cases outside these limits are heard before High Court judges, sitting either in Crown courts in first-tier centres or in the High Court itself.

The High Court of Justice is divided into the Chancery Division, the Queen's Bench Division and the Family Division. Until the Administration of Justice Act 1970 the third division was Probate, Divorce and Admiralty, strange bed-fellows, but with the common factor that the cases they heard were originally all based on Roman Law. The Family Division of the High Court now deals with all jurisdiction affecting the family: divorce, wardship, guardianship and probate (the ratification of wills). Maritime law is the responsibility of a specially constituted court of the Queen's Bench Division. Although the jurisdiction of the High Court in general covers all civil and some criminal matters, the work is shared out among the different divisions. In the same way, although the sixty-eight puisne judges of the High Court can in theory sit in any division, in practice they are all assigned to a particular one.

The Lord Chancellor (see also p. 43) is President of the Court of Appeal and the Chancery Division. At the head of the Queen's Bench Division is the Lord Chief Justice of England, who is next to the Lord Chancellor in the legal hierarchy. The most important judge in the Family Division is the President.

High Court judges sit alone when hearing cases of first instance. Appeals from inferior courts are heard by between one and three judges nominated by the Lord Chancellor. Appeals from the High Court and county courts are heard by the Court of Appeal (Civil Division). The Lord Chancellor, the Lord Chief Justice, the President of the Family Division and the Master of the Rolls are *ex officio* members of this; the ordinary members are fourteen Justices of Appeal.

A case which has been dismissed by the Appeal Court can, with the permission of the Appeal Court, be taken to the House of Lords. In a case at which an important legal principle is at stake the Lords can give permission for an appeal, even if the Appeal Court has not done so. The judicial function of the House of Lords is vested in the ten Lords of Appeal in Ordinary, under the presidency of the Lord Chancellor. The quorum is three, although it is usual for a group of five or seven law lords to hear a case.

Most civil disputes are settled by the respective solicitors (see p. 61) before the case comes to court. When matters cannot be settled amicably 'out of court', however, expensive litigation ensues. An action is usually started by the plaintiff (the aggrieved person) serving a 'writ of summons' on the defendant. This writ informs the defendant that the plaintiff has a claim against him or her and sets down what that claim is. If the defendant intends to defend the case by contesting the claim, he or she 'enters an appearance' by informing the court of his or her intention, and the relevant documents are then sent to the court. Anyone not wishing to go to the trouble and expense of bringing a court case can, if the other party agrees, have a commercial dispute settled by arbitration.

Civil actions are for the most part tried by a judge sitting without a jury. In the case of actions such as defamation (of character) or false imprisonment, however, either party to the dispute can request a trial by jury. When a jury is present it decides not only questions of fact, but also the amount of damages to be awarded. As juries sometimes award damages out of all proportion to what is justified, it has been suggested that the responsibility for assessing damages should be given to the judge, as it is in other civil cases where there is no jury present. The court is also responsible for deciding who should pay the costs of an action, a question of the greatest importance as litigation is extremely expensive. In general the loser may expect to pay the costs of both sides, although in many cases the winner has to meet some of his or her expenses, even when a costs order is given in his or her favour.

Because of the high cost of going to law it has been suggested at various times that small claims courts should be introduced to deal with cases involving relatively small amounts of money. There are now three experimental small claims courts in England, where arbitrators try to work out a solution satisfactory to both sides. The system is entirely voluntary, but once both sides have agreed to accept the arbitrator's decision they are bound to do so. The decision is enforceable in the county court. Similar schemes have been introduced in other places.

OTHER COURTS

Coroners' courts, presided over by a lawyer or a doctor, are common law courts, which are called when someone dies in suspicious circumstances. The coroner's task is to establish the cause of death, and in cases involving violent death an inquest must be held. Administrative tribunals exist outside the hierarchy of the courts and are set up by Act of Parliament or other statute. Examples of administrative tribunals include the Lands Tribunal, which deals with property values, and rent tribunals, which are concerned with determining fair rents.

The Legal Profession

The legal profession has two branches: barristers (known as advocates in Scotland) and solicitors.

SOLICITORS
If a person requires legal advice he or she will go to a solicitor, who for a fee will provide the guidance required and advise on a course of action. Much of the work carried out by a solicitor concerns routine matters, such as buying and selling houses, executing wills and checking documents and contracts, but solicitors are also involved in both criminal and civil cases in courts of law. Normally a person accused of a crime or sued for damages will seek the assistance of a solicitor, who will explain the legal issues involved and take whatever action is necessary on behalf of his or her client. A solicitor is not permitted to plead in the higher courts, so if the case is to be heard in one of these he or she must brief a barrister on the client's behalf.

In order to become a solicitor it is necessary to take 'articles of clerkship' (serve an apprenticeship) with an established solicitor for a period of between two and five years. The actual time spent as an articled clerk depends on the educational qualifications of the individual. A university degree in law, for example, provides exemption from certain examinations. However, in order to qualify as a solicitor, an articled clerk must pass the Law Society examinations. Once this has been done he or she becomes a member of the Law Society, the professional organisation for solicitors in England and Wales.

BARRISTERS
The barrister (who has the right of audience before any court or tribunal in England) conducts proceedings in higher courts and also advises on legal problems that have been submitted by solicitors. It is not customary for a prospective client to approach a barrister directly. As we have seen the solicitor acts as intermediary. In order to become a barrister it is necessary to have reached a certain educational

standard and to have passed an examination set by the Council of Legal Education. A prospective barrister must gain admittance to one of the four Inns of Court: Lincoln's Inn, the Inner Temple, the Middle Temple, or Gray's Inn. Before being 'called to the Bar', that is being accepted as a barrister, the candidate must 'keep' eight terms at the Inn. This means that he or she must dine in the company of fellow members at the Inn a specified number of times and also pass the Bar examinations. After being 'called' the new barrister is expected to keep another four terms and gain experience under the supervision of a practising barrister.

A barrister who has built up a substantial practice as a 'junior' may be tempted to 'take silk' and become a 'Queen's Counsel' (QC) by applying to the Lord Chancellor for a patent. While this will mean higher fees than a junior would receive, the QC is excluded from appearing in less important, but still financially rewarding, cases. However a successful QC can command large fees and will also enjoy considerable prestige both within the legal fraternity and outside. It is also a logical step up the ladder for an ambitious lawyer, for most of the higher judicial offices are held by QCs.

Recently there has been a certain amount of criticism of the legal profession, perhaps the most serious being the charge that by operating a 'closed shop' both solicitors and barristers can claim exorbitant fees. The lawyers reply to charges such as this by pointing out that interpretation of the law is a highly complex business, requiring a great deal of highly skilled work. While this may well be true, in many cases the expense of retaining a solicitor, and perhaps a junior barrister and a QC, means that the costs of litigation are too high for the average person. This may be a good thing in that it prevents the law courts being jammed with a large number of trivial cases, but it also means that a person with a legitimate case can be deprived of justice because the cost of obtaining this justice is so high.

An area that has long been a source of irritation has been that of conveyancing – the transfer of the legal title of a house when someone sells. For years this has been a solicitor's monopoly and many firms have charged fees that were thought to be out of all proportion to the work done. During the last few years there has been a great deal of discussion both within and without the legal profession on this matter, and there has been some movement towards reform. The scale of fees has been scrapped so that it is up to individual firms to fix their rates and the introduction of 'licensed conveyancers' – agents with no legal training, in the sense that solicitors have, but with expertise in conveyancing – has been encouraged in some quarters.

It is also interesting to note that criticism has not only come from outside the legal profession, and that there is a sizeable body of opinion, particularly among younger solicitors, who feel that the distinction between barristers and solicitors is an unreal one in modern times.

In order to get over some of the difficulties of the high cost of going to law, provision has been made for legal aid to be granted in both civil and criminal cases. Legal aid in criminal cases is usually granted at the discretion of the court, and in most cases the defendant will be expected to make some contribution towards the cost of his or her lawyers. In civil cases only applicants with very low incomes qualify for free legal aid. In 1972 a new scheme was announced under which people with low incomes could obtain the services of a solicitor up to the value of £25. Under the Police and Criminal Evidence Act there is a statutory right for people taken to police stations in connection with a criminal offence to be given free legal advice from solicitors.

JUDGES
The English judiciary prides itself on its impartiality and its freedom from political involvement. Judges are appointed by the Lord Chancellor, the senior judge in the country and head of the legal profession, from the senior members of the Bar (or Recorders from Crown courts), and they are non-political appointments. On a number of occasions judges have made legal decisions that have proved acutely embarrassing to the government of the day, for Acts of Parliament that have been ambiguously drafted may be interpreted by the courts in a manner far different from that intended by legislators.

The only way to remove a member of the bench is by a petition to Parliament. As there is no official retiring age for judges there is a danger that some of them may go on exercising their judicial functions when their intellectual powers have begun to decline. There is also a tendency for some of them to take advantage of their position to pontificate on what they consider to be the evils of modern society.

There has also been criticism of the fact that judges are responsible for passing sentences even when they have very little knowledge of the defendant's background, or of the nature of the punishment they are prescribing. As judges are trained solely as lawyers they may have little knowledge of psychology or criminology, and may indeed be rather critical when experts in these sciences appear in court as witnesses.

As we have seen, when barristers 'take silk' they become a Queen's Counsel, which gives the right to use the letters QC, for example Peter Brown QC. Should he then be selected as a 'circuit judge', he will be known as 'His Honour Judge Brown'. If, on the other hand, he becomes a judge in the High Court, he will be referred to as 'The Honourable Mr Justice Brown', and he will also be knighted. If he is promoted to the Appeal Court he will be addressed as 'Lord Justice Brown' (although he is not a member of the peerage) or the 'Right Honourable Sir Peter Brown'. As a 'Lord of Appeal in Ordinary' he would become a life peer with a seat in the Lords and the title of 'The Right Honourable Lord Brown'.

The Jury

The modern jury in England and Wales consists of twelve men or women, between the ages of 18 and 65. They have the responsibility of deciding whether their fellow citizen who is on trial is innocent or guilty of the offence of which he or she is accused. After hearing all the evidence in the case the jury listen to the judge's summing up, and then withdraw to consider their verdict, but the law now allows for majority verdicts, provided there are no more than two dissentients in a jury of twelve. Should a jury be unable to agree a new trial must be held, although in practice this rarely happens. Juries serve in both criminal and civil courts, deciding questions of fact and, in the case of the former, the damages that should be paid to the injured party. Juries do not fix penalties, although in the days when the death penalty was still in force for murder the jury might make a plea for leniency for someone who was likely to be condemned to death as a result of a verdict of 'guilty'.

There are those who claim that the whole concept of the jury is out of date, and that trial by jury should be replaced by trial by experts, as in fact happens in the civil cases where a judge sits alone. Critics of the jury system point to the extravagant damages that juries sometimes award in civil cases. They also claim that juries are subject to prejudices to such an extent that many verdicts are decided almost before the first evidence is presented, particularly in cases involving crimes against the person. The, juror is, of course, supposed to be completely impartial and to have no advance knowledge of the case, but it is very difficult to secure these conditions. Another criticism of juries is that it is easy for organised criminal gangs to bribe or threaten jurors in order to influence their verdicts. In the days when unanimous verdicts were required it was only necessary for one member of the jury to be intimidated to make it impossible to obtain a verdict.

Scotland

As Scotland was an independent kingdom until 1707 its legal system differs from that of England and Wales in a number of respects. However, since the early eighteenth century many of the statutes introduced by Parliament also apply to Scotland, which means that in many cases Scottish law is in line with that of England and Wales. Nevertheless, differences of organisation and procedure are still marked, while sometimes a law that exists in England and Wales may not apply in Scotland and vice versa.

THE SCOTTISH COURTS
The courts of summary jurisdiction in Scotland are the burgh (or police) courts, presided over by town councillors, and the Justice of the Peace courts, which are found outside urban areas and are presided over by judges, sitting in their capacity as Justices of the Peace. Sheriff courts, which serve counties or combinations of counties known as 'sheriffdoms', hear both civil and criminal cases. The supreme criminal court of first instance (that is, the court that tries and sentences an offender) is the High Court of Judiciary. Cases in the High Court are heard by the Lord Justice General, the Lord Justice Clerk or one of the Lords Commissioner of Justiciary. The court is based in Edinburgh, but the judges also go on circuit. Appeals in criminal cases are made to the High Court. There is no appeal to the House of Lords.

The main courts of civil jurisdiction in Scotland are the sheriff courts, while the highest civil court is the Court of Session. The sheriff courts can handle virtually all cases, actions being heard by the sheriff. Appeals can be made to the Sheriff-Principal (the leading sheriff in a sheriffdom) or to the Court of Session. The Court of Session has two parts, an Outer and an Inner House, the former being a court of first instance, the latter mainly an appeal court. From the Inner House an appeal can be made to the House of Lords.

The Police

In 1957 there were 126 police forces in England and Wales and 20 in Scotland. They ranged in size from the Metropolitan Police Force, responsible for policing Greater London, which had 16,419 officers, to one of the Scottish forces which had 16. During the 1960s, largely as a result of recommendations made by the Royal Commission on the Police which reported in 1962, a large number of amalgamations took place. In 1986 there were 52 police forces in Britain, most of them established on a county basis.

The oldest police force in the country is the Metropolitan Police, founded by Sir Robert Peel, then Home Secretary, in 1829. Peel's men were responsible for maintaining order in the capital, and although distrusted and reviled at first, they soon became so successful that they were imitated in other parts of the country. Whereas the Metropolitan Police Force was responsible to the Home Secretary, police forces in other areas were established by local bodies. Although proposals have been made at times that a national force should be set up, there has been little support for the idea from either police or public. At the present time each local force is maintained by a police authority, made up of representatives of the councils covered by the force, and local magistrates. It is the responsibility of the police authority to appoint a chief constable and his immediate subordinates and to provide the equipment to enable the police to carry out their duties. The Home Secretary in England and Wales and the Secretary of State for Scotland exercise a certain amount of control over police forces, by having the final say in the appointment of chief constables and making general regulations covering administration, pay and terms of service. They also appoint the chief inspectors of constabulary, who with their deputies are responsible for inspecting the forces throughout the country (outside London), reporting back to the appropriate Secretary of State.

The relations between police and public, particularly in inner city areas, have aroused a great deal of discussion over the last decade and attempts have been made to introduce new methods of policing and also to ensure that police forces are made accountable. Riots in a number of cities, such as Bristol, Birmingham and several parts of London, together with the police tactics during the miners' strike of 1984/5, alarmed many people who felt that the existing control systems were inadequate. In 1985 a new complaints procedure was established which, for the first time, took the adjudication of disciplinary proceedings out of the hands of the police forces themselves and put them into the hands of the new Police Complaints Authority.

5

The Welfare State

It was not until relatively recently that society felt that it had an obligation to provide protection for those of its members who were sick, old, unemployed or suffering from some other form of deprivation or hardship. During the Middle Ages the feudal system in rural areas and the 'guilds' in the towns provided some degree of protection. In country districts every man had an overlord who looked after the interests of his underlings, although, of course, the feudal system was heavily weighted in favour of the upper classes. The rights of serfs were either very limited or nonexistent. In towns the guilds, which were established to protect the standards of certain trades and to regulate admission to the ranks of skilled craftsmen, also gave assistance to members who were in difficulties. For the destitute and landless there was little or no provision; they were dependent on alms from those who were more fortunate than they, or from the monasteries and convents.

During Tudor times some attempts were made to deal with the problem of the poor and unemployed. At the end of Elizabeth I's reign a Poor Law was passed, and this was to remain the backbone of social legislation in England until 1834, when the Poor Law Amendment Act was introduced. The Poor Law was, as it was intended to be, a harsh Act, designed as much as anything to discourage people from relying on public funds. The fact that the Poor Law remained basically unchanged for over two hundred years is not a testimony to its humanity and effectiveness – rather it shows the attitude of the times. In the opinion of most leading politicians, industrialists, landowners and churchmen, it was not the business of the government to interfere with the running of factories and mines or the building of houses. According to this attitude, poverty was not the result of low wages but of fecklessness and a lack of incentive to work. So industrialists of the eighteenth and early nineteenth centuries continued to build insanitary houses for their workers, forced them to work long hours in shocking conditions and paid them minimal wages. In all this they were aided and abetted by governments which refused to permit working men to organise and to form trade unions to protest against their conditions.

Although a number of important and beneficial reforms were introduced during the first decade of the nineteenth century, they were conceived in a paternalistic manner, while the attitude that poverty was the fault of the poor was still very much in evidence. Nowhere is this more clearly seen than in the Poor Law Amendment Act of 1834, which set up workhouses in place of the 'outdoor relief' introduced by the Elizabethan Poor Law. The theory behind the workhouses was that conditions inside their walls should be more unpleasant than any work available outside, thereby discouraging all but the completely destitute from entering the institution. The harsh regime of the workhouse was designed to stop able-bodied but lazy men from going on relief, but in practice all the inmates had to suffer the strict rules, which led to the separation of families, inadequate food (Oliver Twist was not the only one who wanted more) and insanitary conditions. It is not surprising that before long the workhouse came to be regarded with fear and loathing by the poor, to be avoided at all costs.

Because of the failure of the state to provide security against sickness or unemployment, except in the form of the workhouse, by the middle of the nineteenth century a number of Friendly Societies had been formed. These societies provided financial assistance and medical care in cases of sickness and also a funeral grant so that members who died could avoid the indignity of a pauper burial.

Another area where the authorities were slow to act was public health. In spite of the fact that towns were increasing in size at a prodigious rate at the end of the eighteenth and beginning of the nineteenth centuries, there were few regulations governing building standards. The result was that slums of 'back-to-back' houses, without proper drainage or ventilation, became commonplace in many industrial cities. Cramped living conditions and indifference to proper methods of rubbish and sewage disposal led to a number of serious outbreaks of infectious disease during the nineteenth century, for example, cholera in 1831–2 and 1848–9, and smallpox in 1881. Following the first cholera epidemic a number of towns established boards of health, but it was not until the Public Health Act of 1848 that a national General Board of Health was set up. In 1875 a second Public Health Act introduced a nation-wide system of public health, under the control of the Local

Government Board. In the same year an Act was passed which provided for the clearance of slum districts, while a number of other Acts of the 1870s and 1880s relating to education, trade unions and housing showed that the government was belatedly recognising that it had responsibilities towards the community as a whole.

By the end of the nineteenth century there were a number of Acts providing protection from the worst excesses of the industrial system. However, it should be stressed that many of the Acts had only been accepted after a long and bitter struggle both inside and outside Parliament. The social legislation of the nineteenth century was in most cases the work of a few men and women who had to struggle against the indifference, and frequently the hostility, of parliamentarians of both parties.

Between 1906 and 1914 the Liberal Party was instrumental in introducing a far-reaching programme of social reform. Here again the question of motives arises. Opinions differ as to how far the Liberals were really interested in improving the welfare of the less well-off members of society, and how far they were continuing the paternalism of the previous century. Whatever the motives behind the reforms introduced by the Liberal administration that held office in the years before the First World War, they were to have considerable impact on the country. Particularly important were the Old Age Pensions Act of 1908 and the National Insurance Act of 1911. Other measures included the setting up of labour exchanges, legislation to improve the position of trade unionists and a minimum wage for coal miners. Reforms affecting education covered the provision of school meals and a medical service for schoolchildren.

Despite reforms such as these, up until the First World War the government intervened very little in the life of the average citizen. Many people were totally unaffected by the welfare legislation just described, while some still regarded the provision of aid to the unemployed and sick as aiding and abetting laziness and dishonesty. During the war the government became much more involved in the personal life of citizens, as virtually the whole country was mobilised to meet the threat of total war. Regulations were introduced which affected the whole population, including the Defence of the Realm Act, which gave the government powers that were almost dictatorial in the interests of safeguarding the country and winning the war.

After the war the state's powers of intervention were cut back to some extent, but there was no return to the conditions of 1914. For some, Lloyd George's promises to build a country 'fit for heroes to live in' implied that a far-reaching programme of social reform would be undertaken; but in spite of a widening of the scope of the National Insurance Act, and legislation to build more houses, developments during the interwar years were disappointing. Indeed the economic crises of the 1920s and 1930s showed only too clearly that the action taken to provide unemployment benefits was of limited value when it was a question of dealing with 2 or 3 million workers without jobs. Housing was provided by local councils at cheap rents that were subsidised by the state, but even so demand outstripped supply, and housing conditions in many industrial cities were extremely poor at this time.

It was during the Second World War that the blueprint for the welfare state was produced by a committee under the chairmanship of Sir William Beveridge. The Beveridge Report, published in 1942, outlined a comprehensive scheme of social security, designed, as Beveridge said, to attack want, disease, ignorance, squalor and idleness. The Beveridge plan proposed a complete break with the old Poor Law outlook which was still prevalent in British welfare circles, and the substitition of an entirely new concept. The plan was 'first and foremost a plan of insurance', towards which individuals paid a contribution, and from which they received benefits when needed, as of right. The plan also provided for child allowances, a national health service and an end to mass unemployment. There was a tremendous public response to the plan, and in 1944 a draft Bill was published. A Ministry of National Insurance was set up in the same year. In June 1945 Churchill's caretaker Government passed a Family Allowances Act, but as it was defeated at the general election in October it was unable to follow this up with further legislation.

The Labour Party had accepted the main principles of the Beveridge Report shortly after it was published and after coming to power they lost little time in introducing the necessary legislation. The Family Allowances Act already mentioned came into effect in August 1946 and provided a weekly allowance of 5 shillings (25p) for every child except the first. The allowance was available to all, but as it was taxable it meant that people with larger incomes received little or no benefit. The family allowance is now known as child benefit; it is paid for all children under the age of 16, and in 1985 was paid at the rate of £7.00 per week.

The National Insurance (Industrial Injuries) Act provided compensation for those injured at work, but was to a large extent overshadowed by the main National Insurance Act which became law in 1946. By the terms of this Act the entire adult population, that is everybody between the school-leaving age of 15 and the retirement age of 65, was compulsorily insured for sickness benefit, unemployment benefit, retirement pension, widow's pension, maternity grants and allowances, and death grants. As in the case of the 1911 Act, contributions came from employee, employer (except of course in the case of self-employed and non-employed persons) and the state. But the contributions were to be administered by the recently established Ministry of National Insurance (now the Department of Health and Social Security), not by Friendly Societies and insurance companies as previously.

The National Health Act was also passed in 1946, although it did not begin to operate until July 1948. Its aim was to provide the nation with a complete range of medical services, including those of specialists, dentists and hospital staff, as far as possible without charge to the patient. The cost of the National Health Service (the NHS) was to be met out of general taxation, while a proportion of the receipts from national insurance would also contribute towards its upkeep. The Act had far-reaching implications, for by providing, or seeking to provide, a comprehensive service for every member of the community, it completely changed the structure of medical care in the United Kingdom.

Hospitals which had previously been administered by local authorities or voluntary societies were brought under the control of fourteen regional hospital boards in England and Wales. In Scotland and Northern Ireland complementary but distinct National Health Acts established hospital boards, five in the former and one in the latter area. The day-to-day running of hospitals was made the responsibility of hospital management committees, with overall control being exercised by the Minister of Health. The original Bill had proposed that doctors should come under the control of local authorities, but the doctors' professional organisation, the British Medical Association, protested so violently about this idea that executive councils were established instead. The 138 councils were responsible under the Ministry of Health for keeping records, paying doctors and dentists for their services and for overseeing the running of the 'Family Practitioner Services.' at the local level. The third main division of the NHS was the local health services, which provided facilities for the maintenance of health. These local health services included home nursing, child welfare, health visiting and ambulances.

A year after the NHS was introduced it covered 95 per cent of the population and cost almost £400 million a year to run. By the mid-1980s the cost of running the NHS had risen to over £16,000 million a year. In 1984, 6,180,000 people were treated as hospital in-patients, with nearly 40,000,000 out-patient attendances.

Although when the NHS was introduced it was intended that treatment and medicines would be provided without extra charge to patients, later some charges were introduced for medicines. This was bitterly opposed by the left wing of the Labour Party, who felt that the basic concept of the NHS was being undermined. At the present time a charge is made for medicines and some forms of treatment, for example dental care, but certain categories of patient, such as pregnant women, are exempt from charges. In cases of hardship or prolonged illness, medicines are free.

The Poor Law was finally brought to an end legally in 1948, although in practice it had ceased to function during the 1930s when the number of unemployed was so great that the guardians could not meet their responsibilities. The National Assistance Act of 1948 set up the National Assistance Board which was designed to aid those in need. Basic rates of assistance were laid down by the national government, though individual offices were given discretionary powers.

The Welfare State Today

THE NATIONAL HEALTH SERVICE

The NHS has come in for considerable criticism during its few decades of existence. In the opinion of many people its objectives are too ambitious for the limited funds that are available, and the press and other media are constantly forecasting its imminent collapse. Nor are criticisms confined to those outside the Health Service: doctors, nurses, radiographers and others who work in hospitals and elsewhere have on many occasions expressed their dissatisfaction with the terms of service – particularly rates of pay, level of staffing and the running of the NHS. However while many of these criticisms are undoubtedly founded on fact it does not necessarily follow that the NHS has been a failure. Indeed it can be argued that far from failing, the NHS has been too successful, in that the provision of a wide range of health services at little or no cost has increased consumer demand. Those who pre- viously did not get medical attention are now receiving it and many people who before 1948 would have died are now receiving treatment and being cured.

Not surprisingly attitudes to the NHS follow party political lines. During the 1970s the Labour government attempted to phase out 'pay beds' (that is, beds for the use of 'private' or paying patients), but the policy of the Conservatives, in power since 1979, has been to increase the amount of involvement of the private sector, arguing that by doing this they will relieve the pressure on the NHS. There are some 25,000 general practitioners (GPs or family doctors) in Britain, each with an average of 2,100 patients. National Health hospitals provide about half a million beds and are staffed by some 480,000 doctors and nurses.

Since April 1974, when the National Health Service Reorganisation Act took effect, the NHS has been administered as a single unified service. In place of the regional hospital boards, the executive councils and the personal health services run by local authorities there are in England three levels of planning: regional, area and the central Department. The Secretary of State for Health and Social Security has overall responsibility for policy and for supervising the regional and area authorities. There are fourteen regional health authorities (RHAs), each of which incorporates a university medical school. Members of the RHA are appointed by the Secretary of State in consultation with interested organisations, such as the universities and local authorities. It is the responsibility of the regional authority to act as a link between the Secretary of State and the area authorities, and also to oversee the work done in the region as a whole and in each of the areas for which it is responsible. The boundaries of the area health authorities (AHAs) are for the most part the same as for the major local government authorities which came into being in April 1974. There are ninety AHAs in England (Wales has twelve AHAs and Scotland fifteen health boards which perform similar functions; there are no RHAs outside England). The chairman of each AHA is appointed by the Secretary of State, while the remaining members are appointed by the local authorities, the local university and the RHA. A number of the members of the authority are professionals, for example, doctors and nurses, the others laymen. The AHA is responsible for running the health services in the area for which it is responsible. Doctors, dentists, opticians, pharmacists and others offering professional services remain as independent contractors. In place of the executive councils each AHA has a Family Practitioner Committee consisting of thirty members. Half the committee members are appointed by the interested professions, eleven by the AHA and four by the local authority.

The AHA is the body that puts the NHS into effect, as it is responsible for deciding what the needs of the area are and for meeting these needs. In addition to providing medical staff the AHAs also ensure that there are adequate services to back up the work done in the surgeries and hospitals. The AHA is divided into districts, each of which has a population of between 200,000 and 500,000. The number of districts is decided by the AHA. While some areas contain only one district, others that are more populous may have up to five.

In 1970 the Local Authority Social Services Act enabled county councils, county borough and London boroughs to set up social services departments to integrate the personal social services. The welfare of young people, juvenile offenders, the physically handicapped, the mentally ill, the elderly and the homeless are all the concern of the local authority social services departments. The facilities provided by the NHS and those of the local authorities are intended to complement each other.

SOCIAL SECURITY

The range of benefits available to people living in Britain today fall into two main categories: contributory and non-contributory. Contributory benefits depend on prior payments to the National Insurance scheme and include retirement, sickness and invalidity benefit, unemployment benefit and maternity allowance. Non-contributory benefits are financed by general taxation revenue and cover supplementary benefit, family income supplement and housing benefit.

Every working person over the minimum school-leaving age (16) must make a weekly national insurance contribution. Contributions are also paid by employers and the government. The main benefits paid under the National Insurance scheme are: retirement pensions – £38·30 per week in November 1985 – paid to men at the age of 65 and women at the age of 60; maternity allowance – £29·15 per week for 18 weeks; child benefit – paid at the rate of £7·00 per week to mothers of all children up to the age of 16; sickness benefit – £29·15 per week for up to 28 weeks off work – and disability benefit; and unemployment benefit – payable at a rate of £30·45 a week for up to a year.

Non-contributory benefits are primarily intended to ensure that those with low or irregular incomes are able to provide for themselves and their families. Supplementary benefits are paid to people over the age of 16 who are either unemployed or working less than thirty hours a week who have insufficient money to support themselves. In November 1985 supplementary benefit was paid at the following rates: £47·85 for a married couple, and £29·50 for a person living alone; the long-term rates were £60·00 and £37·50 respectively. Although people with low incomes have a legal right to supplementary benefit large numbers do not claim it. Many people, particularly pensioners, regard the payments as charity, while others object to having a means test (a device whereby the authorities investigate the income and savings of applicants). Still others do not know how to claim or are worried by the bureaucracy involved. Recipients of supplementary benefit are also entitled to other benefits, such as assistance with housing, school meals, and so on. People in low income jobs bringing up children are entitled to claim family income supplement (FIS) until the child is 16 (or 19 if still at school). FIS, which like supplementary benefit is subject to a means test, is granted on an annual basis, but it can be reapplied for.

In December 1985 the Government published a White Paper proposing far-reaching changes in the structure of the Welfare State, particularly in the areas of pensions, family support, and housing and discretionary grants. The proposals were immediately attacked by many who felt that they undermined the basis of the Welfare State.

Housing

For the average Englishman (and his cousins elsewhere in the British Isles) the only real home is a house. It is estimated that over 80 per cent of the population of Britain live in houses or bungalows, the remainder in flats or maisonettes. A house can be detached, semi-detached, or in a terrace, but ideally should stand in its own garden and have both a front and a back door. Although the bungalow has become increasingly popular in recent years, the traditional British house has two storeys, the bottom one containing the living rooms (or in the language of the estate agent the 'reception rooms'), and kitchen, and the upper floor the bedrooms and bathroom. The average house built in this century has two living rooms and two or three bedrooms, and there is often storage space in the form of a pantry (for food) or cupboards. The commonest building material is brick, although many of the houses built in the last three decades use prefabricated techniques, employing concrete, plastics and other modern materials.

It is estimated that there are more than 20 million homes in the United Kingdom. About half of these are owner-occupied, a third are rented from local authorities, while the rest are rented from private landlords. In 1980 the government introduced a scheme under which tenants living in council houses could buy their homes and about half a million did so. (An estimated 200,000 families, that is, about 1 per cent of the population, have two homes.) As few people have sufficient money to purchase a home outright, the usual procedure is to take a loan in the form of a mortgage from a building society, bank or other financial institution, or a local authority. This long-term loan, which is usually paid back over a period of twenty or twenty-five years, is given at a comparatively low rate of interest, although over the last twenty years interest rates have risen considerably. In 1964 the standard rate was 6 per cent, ten years later it had risen to 11 per cent, while in late 1986 it was 12·25 per cent. The bulk of mortgage finance is still provided by one of the 350 or so building societies, but during the 1970s a number of banks also entered the mortgage market, probably due to the fact that a spectacular rise in house prices at the beginning of the decade made mortgage funds scarce. It is estimated that in 1972–3 house prices went up by 50 per cent in a period of eighteen months in the London area. This rise in prices continued, albeit at a more modest level, throughout the decade, and in 1985 it was estimated by the Anglia Building Society that the average price of a three-bedroomed, semi-detached house (that is, a house split into two living units) was £23,850 in the north-east, £41,000 in the south-east and £57,170 in the Greater London area. Owner-occupiers are entitled to tax relief on interest payments on the first £30,000 of their mortgage, although there have been suggestions from some quarters that this concession should be phased out.

About 40 per cent of Britain's housing stock has been built since the Second World War, and until the late 1970s a significant proportion of the new housing stock was provided by local authorities. Since 1979, however, the policy of the Government has been to encourage private rather than public building of residential property, while in 1980 a scheme was started whereby council tenants were entitled to buy their homes.

Adequate housing has been a problem for many years, and is made worse by the fact that many of the worst houses are privately owned by landlords who have little incentive to provide improved conditions for their tenants. Until 1957 rents were controlled, but in that year a Rent

Act was passed which permitted rents to rise at the same rate as prices. The declared aim behind this Act was to make it financially attractive for people to buy property for renting. It was hoped that more dwellings would thus become available and the housing shortage would be eased. However, the Act introduced a number of new problems, one of which was that while 'sitting tenants' were permitted to retain their tenancies without an increase in rent, new tenants could be charged at a higher rate. This situation meant that people whose interest lay in making money, rather than helping with the housing problem, could make a lucrative business out of buying up large houses with several 'sitting tenants' cheaply, and then forcing these tenants out. The house, minus tenants, could then be sold at a considerable profit. In 1965 a further Rent Act was introduced, restoring security of tenure for tenants and providing strong penalties for harassment. The basis of the new Act was a 'regulated tenancy', fixed at a 'fair rent' by a rent officer. Should the landlord or tenant object to the rent officer's decision, the case could go to the rent assessment committee for consideration. Once a rent had been fixed it would remain in force for three years. In 1974 the provisions of the Rent Act were extended to include furnished accommodation. In 1980 the Housing Act, which gave council tenants the right to buy their home, also altered the provisions of the Rent Act by introducing a system of 'shorthold' lettings, giving tenants security of tenure for an agreed period but not for life.

Housing societies, which build dwellings for co-ownership or to let, have become widespread following the establishment of the Housing Corporation in 1964. It is estimated that the 3,000 or so housing societies and associations own about 500,000 homes in England and Wales. Housing societies are financed by building societies and the Housing Corporation, each of which provides 50 per cent of the money needed for building.

In spite of the fact that the people of Britain are better housed today than at any other time in their history, the problem of housing is still a major one. An estimated 37 per cent of the housing stock was built before 1919. While much of this is in good condition, particularly in country areas where possession of an old (but modernised) country cottage is regarded as a status symbol, and in residential suburbs, there are many urban areas where bad conditions still exist. There are also a depressingly large number of people who do not have homes of any kind, and who have to rely on hostels provided by local authorities, many of which are reminiscent of the workhouses of the last century.

One body that has been actively fighting poor housing conditions and the problems of the homeless is Shelter, which has branches in many large towns. There are many people who feel that the provision of housing is not the responsibility of the state or local authorities, and that individuals should make their own arrangements. However, as we have seen, it is difficult for those with low salaries to qualify for a building society mortgage unless they can produce a large deposit from their savings. Housing is always one of the most important issues in elections, at both local and national level. There is little doubt that with the very large increases in the price of houses in recent years the problem will continue to be a pressing one.

6

Education

Schools

The English education system has always tended to resemble a handicap race. However, whereas in the usual form of handicap race the aim is to give all competitors an equal chance of winning by placing some impediment on those who have an advantage, the aim of the English school system seems to be to give those who have an advantage an even greater one.

The first English schools were founded by the church in the sixth century, to train boys for the priesthood, and the church was to retain a virtual monopoly of education for many centuries. During the Middle Ages most of the schools that existed were attached to cathedrals, monasteries or collegiate churches, although they were sometimes supplemented by establishments founded and endowed by rich burgesses for the education of their sons. The state played virtually no part in education. Although individual monarchs could follow the example of Alfred the Great and establish particular institutions, as Henry VI did in the case of Eton, the state accepted no responsibility for either organising or financing any educational system. During Tudor times a number of schools were established; Edward VI founded some dozen schools, still known as King Edward VI Grammar Schools, while a number of others opened their doors in Elizabeth I's reign.

Education was the prerogative of the rich. Although scholarships existed for 'poor and needy' boys who showed an aptitude for learning, there were not nearly enough of them to provide places for all those having this qualification. If a child did not attend school he or she might pick up the rudiments of reading and writing from a parent, relative, or neighbour, but in many cases people were illiterate for life. A number of the giants of the Industrial Revolution had received little or no formal education: James Brindley, the great canal engineer, taught himself to write in order to be able to keep his notebooks up to date, while the older Stephenson, of 'Rocket' fame, was illiterate to manhood.

During the late eighteenth century a considerable number of 'industrial schools' and 'Sunday schools' were established by industrialists and philanthropists. These institutions were intended to provide a basic education for the working class or at least what their founders considered to be a basic education. The men who set up these schools were not particularly concerned about training future Brindleys and Stephensons to read plans and technical works; they were more anxious to ensure that their workers could read the Bible. Thus the main emphasis was to provide a man or child with enough reading knowledge to stumble through the scriptures, while arithmetic, writing and other potentially dangerous subjects were practically ignored. One of the great problems of these early schools was a shortage of trained teachers, for frequently parents as well as children crowded into the classrooms.

At the beginning of the nineteenth century such elementary schools as existed were financed either by private individuals or the churches. Local authorities were empowered to make grants towards education from the rates if they saw fit to do so, but by no means all of them did. The Church of England no longer had the monopoly of education it had enjoyed in earlier times, and frequently found itself in conflict with Nonconformists over which church should have the right to provide education in a particular area. At times the issue became so heated, and the opponents so involved in questions of principle, that the children were completely forgotten and remained uneducated.

If the churches wanted to fight over the right to educate the young, the state for its part seemed indifferent. This aloofness was to continue until 1833, when Parliament made a grant of £20,000 for the provision of 'school houses'. Although this grant could hardly be described as generous, it did mark the beginning of the state's involvement in education, which was to increase throughout the century, culminating in the Education Act of 1870. This Act, often known as the Forster Act after the man who piloted it through Parliament, established some 300 school boards throughout the country which were empowered to provide schools for elementary education in their respective areas. By the end of the decade a national system of education had been established, providing free compulsory education for all children between the ages of 5 and 10 (14 by 1900).

Although elementary education for all had been achieved, secondary education was still the privilege of those who were able to pay for it. The nineteenth century saw a revival of the ancient secondary schools, many of which received new endowments, enabling them to expand and enlarge their intake of pupils – fee-paying, of course. In addition to the revival of the old-established schools, many new ones were founded. Like their predecessors, they provided an exclusive education, based on the classics, for members of the middle and upper classes. The Victorian public school – 'public' then, as now, meant 'private' – was, however, much more than mere bricks and mortar. It quickly became the training ground for the men who were to rule Britain and the Empire. At the beginning of the century most of the public schools were in a bad way. Neither the masters nor the pupils seemed to have much interest in education, while discipline was so bad that on one occasion the military were called in to suppress a riot at one of the best-known schools. Under the influence of such men as Samuel Butler and Thomas Arnold, however, things began to change. Butler revised the syllabus at his school, Shrewsbury, placing an emphasis on a liberal education; while at Rugby, Arnold laid the foundations of the public schools' role as institutions where boys were trained to be Christian gentlemen. A Royal Commission appointed to report on seven of the most prestigious schools in 1864 found much to be commended in them, and as a result the position of the public schools was confirmed by the Public Schools Act of 1868.

It was not until the beginning of the twentieth century that an opportunity was provided for children whose parents could not afford expensive school fees to benefit from secondary education. Under the terms of the 1902 Education Act, 25 per cent of the places in secondary schools, excluding public schools, were reserved for scholarship pupils. In 1918 the Fisher Education Act increased the number of secondary schools, but the demand for places still exceeded the supply, and the position did not improve much before the 1940s. But a number of reports had been commissioned between the two world wars, and in 1944 a new Education Act was passed, which reorganised secondary education in England and Wales.

One of the reforms effected by the 1944 (Butler) Act was that the President of the Board of Education was replaced by a Minister of Education. This minister was expected to 'promote the education of the people of England and Wales ... and to secure the effective execution by local authorities ... of the national policy for providing a varied and comprehensive educational service in every area'. This effectively meant that guidelines were drawn up by the ministry, while the individual education authorities decided what form education would take in their area. The Act stipulated that education would be divided into three stages: primary, from 5 to 12; secondary, over 12 to under 19; and further – post-school. The school-leaving age was fixed at 15, with the intention of raising it to 16 when facilities became available. Other important clauses of the Act dealt with the welfare role of local authorities in relation to education, a standardised scale of payment for all teachers employed by local authorities, and a system of inspection for independent schools (those outside the state system).

The 1944 Act defined two kinds of state schools, county and voluntary. The former were provided and maintained by the local authority, while the latter were schools that had been originally founded by the churches. Voluntary schools, the vast majority of which are primary schools, were divided into three categories: 'controlled', 'aided' and 'special agreement'. The distinction between the different categories depends largely on the amount of financial assistance given by the local authority, and the powers the authority and the religious body have over appointing certain members of staff.

The Act paved the way for two kinds of secondary school, the grammar school and the secondary modern school. Some areas had a third type, the secondary technical school, while in other areas the local education authority gained ministry approval for more individual schemes. In Anglesey, in North Wales, for example, a comprehensive system, in which all pupils of secondary school age went to the same kind of school, was instituted. For the majority of pupils, however, the existence of two different kinds of school meant a choice, and in most cases the choice was made on the basis of examination results. The decisive examination, known as the 11-plus, was taken in the last year at the primary school, and its intention was to distinguish between academic and non-academic children. Those who did well in the intelligence and other tests that made up the examination passed and went to grammar schools, while those who failed went to secondary modern schools, where they received a less academic type of education. It was the intention of those who had framed the 1944 Act that there should be 'parity of esteem' between the different kinds of secondary school, that is that the grammar schools should not be considered 'better' in any way than the other schools. However good the intentions of the men and women responsible for the Act, they seem to have failed to take into account the pressures of the postwar social system, and to have totally miscalculated the reactions of parents, teachers and children.

The grammar schools prepared children for the General Certificate of Education (GCE) examinations at Ordinary and Advanced level, which are the qualifications for entry to higher education and the professions. In secondary modern schools, on the other hand, the emphasis was on practical education, leading to skilled or unskilled jobs. It is not surprising therefore that the secondary modern pupil felt himself inferior to the child who went to the grammar school. He qualified for his school by failing an examination, and then found that he was unable to take the later examinations he would need to pass if he wanted to continue into higher education. Many took the Certificate of Education (CSE) which was designed as a 'lower level' GCE 'O level' with less emphasis on academic achievement. Pressure from parents and teachers forced many secondary modern schools to introduce courses leading to GCE examinations, and before long the secondary modern schools in many areas had become imitation grammar schools.

It was this state of affairs, together with growing scepticism about the ability of the 11-plus examination to predict the long-term intellectual ability of the child, that led many educationalists to press for the introduction of comprehensive schools. These were to be non-selective and would provide courses for children of all levels of ability. In spite of the fact that the Labour Government of 1945–51 had accepted the 1944 Act with its principle of selection, during the 1950s attitudes changed, and when the Labour Party returned to power in 1964 it announced that it would introduce a system of comprehensive schools throughout the country.

In 1965 the Secretary of State sent out a circular (Circular 10/65) which invited all local authorities to submit plans for the introduction of comprehensive education. By the beginning of 1970, most of the 163 local education authorities had done so, although some had refused, presumably for political reasons. In February 1970, therefore, the Secretary of State for Education introduced a Bill 'to impose on local authorities a duty to plan for and to achieve a system of comprehensive secondary education'. During the debate on the Bill the Conservative spokesman on education said that if it was passed the Conservatives would repeal it when they returned to power. This, however, proved unnecessary as the Bill did not go through before the 1970 general election. One of the first actions of the incoming Conservative Secretary of State was to withdraw Circular 10/65, and replace it with

Circular 10/70. The new circular stated that the Government felt it was wrong to impose a uniform pattern of secondary education by legislation, and that local authorities should be free to choose the kind of secondary education they considered was best fitted to local needs. In most cases the authorities who had made considerable progress along the road to comprehensive schools decided to continue with their policy. Others who, for one reason or another, had been slower in getting started, announced that they would retain selection. In February 1974, however, a Labour government was once again returned to power and the new Secretary of State for Education announced that it was Labour policy to introduce a fully comprehensive system in England and Wales, if necessary by legislation. Reorganisation continued during the 1970s and although the Conservative Party opposed the measures at both the national and local level it failed to stop the changes in the school structure from being implemented. There were those who hoped that the election of the Thatcher administration in 1979 would halt the process – Mrs Thatcher as Secretary of State for Education in the 1970–4 Heath government had supported the grammar/secondary modern school system – but it was felt that as the introduction of comprehensives had gone so far it should be allowed to continue. In 1985, twenty years after the introduction of Circular 10/65, it was estimated that some 90 per cent of the school population at the secondary stage attended comprehensive schools.

STATE SCHOOLS

Although the comprehensive school is now the 'standard' secondary school in England and Wales, there are marked differences between the schools that the various education authorities elected to set up. Circular 10/65 listed the following types:

(1) The 'all-through school' providing education from 11 to 18.
(2) The two-tier school where children transfer from the primary school to a junior comprehensive or 'middle' school at the age of 11 and then go on to a senior comprehensive at 13 or 14.
(3) The parallel-tiered school where only some children choose or are selected for the upper tier.
(4) The tiered school, where children go from primary school to comprehensive at 11, and then at 13–14 have the option of going to either a senior school taking them past the school-leaving age,

or one that provides education up to the official school-leaving age.

(5) Schools for ages 11–16, followed by sixth-form colleges.
(6) The three-tier system: primary schools from 5 to 8–9; comprehensive school from 8–9 to 12–13; comprehensive senior school from 12 to 13 plus.

The circular tended to favour the 11–18 school, which most closely resembled the age grouping of the grammar and secondary modern schools, but different education authorities have selected different models, depending on how they and their advisers assessed the merits of the various systems. In most comprehensive schools both GCE and CSE courses are offered, though both GCE 'O level' and CSE are due to be phased out in 1988 (see p. 91). One interesting development has been the establishment of sixth-form colleges in many areas, which take children at the post Ordinary Level stage. Students attending these colleges spend two or three years preparing for Advanced level examinations which will give them an opportunity to enter higher education. The establishment of these institutions has been welcomed by those studying at them, as the fact that they are physically separate from the younger children means that the rigorous school regulations governing dress and behaviour can be relaxed and the students can study in an atmosphere that is closer to that of a university than a school.

Many teachers and educationalists who opposed the introduction of comprehensive schools did so, not because they favoured an élite, but because they did not like the way comprehensive schools were being established. The popular view of a comprehensive school is a large purpose-built campus providing a complete range of educational facilities, staffed with sufficient specialists to ensure that the children get the widest possible education, provided in small teaching groups. It is unlikely that even the most impassioned supporter of comprehensive schools could argue that this is always the reality. In many cases the schools, formed by the amalgamation of existing grammar and secondary modern schools, have carried on in the old buildings. Many of these date from the beginning of the century, or even earlier, and often the buildings are separated from each other by busy streets, while in some country areas they are even in different towns.

The restructuring of secondary education in England and Wales inevitably had an effect on the organisation of schools at the pre-secondary stage. Under the system established by the 1944 Act pupils entered primary schools at the age of 5 and then transferred to secondary schools at 11. This system still prevails where the comprehensive school provides education over the age range 11 to 18, but in other areas where middle schools have been established school children move on to comprehensive schools at the age of 12, 13 or 14, according to the system that the local education authority has adopted.

It is estimated that in the mid-1980s over 10 million children aged between 5 and 16 attended Britain's 37,000 schools. In England and Wales there are some 20,000 primary schools, 1,333 middle schools and 3,300 comprehensive schools. In Scotland virtually all the secondary schools are six-year comprehensives, although Northern Ireland retains a selective system.

The Organisation of Schools

Local Education Authorities   One of the reasons for the complexity of the English education system is that the Government is unwilling to intervene directly in education at the local level. As we have seen it was not until 1833 that the Government felt that it was obliged to make any contribution to education at all, and when, in 1870, elementary education was introduced the responsibility for the provision of schools was given to decentralised schools boards throughout the country. The 1902 and 1918 Education Acts made no attempt to centralise control of education, although the 1902 Act reduced the number of local bodies. In 1944 the responsibility for the provision of education was given to 163 local education authorities while, as we have seen, the President of the Board of Education was replaced by a Minister of Education. Twenty years later the Ministry of Education was expanded to include the Ministry for Science, and also to take responsibility for the universities, becoming the Department of Education and Science (DES), headed by a Secretary of State. The Secretary of State is responsible for framing and directing policy, and for the general supervision of the local education authorities, although he or she will not intervene at the local level unless it is felt that the authority is acting unreasonably.

It is often suggested that the English system of local authority control of education has advantages, as the system is more flexible than it would be if schools were directly under the control of a ministry.

There is no central board of education to decide syllabuses, teaching methods and other details, although the DES does lay down minimum standards and gives advice to the local authorities. Contact between the schools and the Secretary of State is maintained by officials known as Her Majesty's Inspectors of Schools (HMIs), who inspect schools and the teaching done in them, and also assist and advise individual teachers. Although as a general rule the syllabus and curriculum of a school are not laid down by statute, there is an exception. According to the 1944 Education Act, every school day must begin with a collective act of worship, and children must be given religious instruction (although parents can withdraw their children from both of these if they so wish).

While local control may have its advantages it can, as we have seen, produce problems. Local authorities are by no means of the same standard when it comes to providing educational facilities. Education can often become a political issue as party politics play an increasingly important part at local government level. This was certainly so in the case of comprehensive schools, particularly in the period between 1964 and 1970 when Conservative-controlled local education authorities tried to resist Labour plans to replace secondary modern schools and grammar schools.

Education committees consist of members of district councils in metropolitan counties and county councils elsewhere, together with co-opted experts (for example, the Professor of Education from the local university). The education committee is appointed by the council, which acts as the local education authority, and is responsible to it. The LEA also appoints a chief education officer, and it is this official who is responsible for administering education on a day-to-day basis in the LEA area. As we have seen, the LEA has the duty of providing primary, local and further education; some higher education, for example that provided by polytechnics, is an LEA responsibility, but universities are not. Education is financed from the rates (see p. 52) and also by a grant from the central government. It is the latter provision that ultimately gives power to the Secretary of State, should he or she choose to use it, for if local authorities refuse to accept directions from central government their funds can be cut off. Although local authorities are expected to provide nursery schools for children over the age of 2, few are able to do this, in spite of the fact that there is considerable demand. For most authorities their responsibility begins when the child goes to primary school at the age of 5. Some primary schools are voluntary schools, originally built and maintained by the churches, but now largely dependent on the local authority for finance. In controlled schools the local authority is responsible for the maintenance of the school buildings, and appoints the majority of the school governors and members of the teaching staff. However, the authority must consult the governors over the appointment of the head teacher and any teacher giving religious instruction. Most of the controlled schools are run by the Church of England. In the case of aided schools the governors are responsible for the fabric (that is, the buildings) of the school, although they can usually obtain financial assistance from the DES. Religious instruction in aided schools is controlled by the managers, two-thirds of whom are appointed by the religious body running the school.

INDEPENDENT SCHOOLS

To many people English education means the public schools, which conjure up an image of boys in striped blazers and straw boaters playing exotic games, and being educated in buildings that are more reminiscent of medieval castles or Victorian railway stations than educational establishments. In fact, in terms of numbers, the public schools comprise a very small minority of the schools in England. Only 5 per cent of the school population receive their education in such institutions. In terms of influence and prestige, however, their importance is very great.

There is no exact definition of a public school, although one thing a public school is *not* is public in the usual sense of the word. Originally 'public' meant that a school was run by a governing body 'in the public interest', as opposed to private schools that were run for the benefit of their proprietor. Today the public schools are usually held to be the two hundred or so schools whose headmasters belong to the Headmasters' Conference (the HMC), although recently the heads of some state schools have been invited to join this body. Traditionally, a school whose headmaster belongs to the HMC must have a certain degree of independence from the state, a sixth form above a certain size, and a good proportion of pupils entering universities each year.

Public schools draw their finances from fees (which, in 1985, averaged £4,200 a year at boarding schools), from trusts and endowments, and from land and property. In recent years a useful source of extra money has been that provided by industry for the building of science laboraries or teaching rooms. Public schools receive no state support and have few scholarship places.

Some public schools are very ancient: Winchester was founded in 1394 and Eton in 1400. But the majority of the schools were established during the nineteenth century to provide secondary education for middle- and upper-class boys, who would go on to the universities of Oxford or Cambridge and thence into the professions or the Church (of England).

Although the number of public schools is very small in comparison with other secondary schools, they have a great influence on society in Britain as a whole. If one looks at the educational background of politicians of all parties, of civil servants, High Court judges, leading Churchmen, prominent industrialists and high-ranking officers in the armed forces, one finds an overwhelming number of public school educated men. The power of the 'old school tie' can play a considerable part in getting a university place, particularly at Oxford and Cambridge, or a certain kind of job. This is not to say that having been to public school guarantees a university place, or a good job, but it does tend to make life easier.

Many public schools are boarding schools and the majority of them are single-sex institutions, catering for boys. There are a number of public-school-type establishments for girls, most of them of recent foundation, and a few co-educational boarding schools, although usually these are rather far removed from the conventional public school idea. Parents wishing their child to enter a public school may have to put his or her name down for the school a number of years before he or she is old enough to go there. Children destined for public schools frequently attend private preparatory (or prep) schools between the ages of 5 and 13, after which they transfer to the public school. A child intending to go to a public school has to sit for the 'Common Entrance' examination. If the child passes this examination, he or she goes to the school which has been chosen. In practice few boys or girls whose parents have the means to send them to a public school fail to gain a place, although this may not always be at the school of their first choice. Factors such as family connections with the school also play a not unimportant part in selection. Not all those intending to go to a public school attend a prep school; some go through the state primary system and then on to a public school, although there are problems here, one being the difference in the age at which transfer is made.

It may seem strange that parents are prepared to pay large school fees every year when it is possible to get free education at the state's expense. Some parents, however, consider that the advantages of the independent schools is such that the money they pay in fees is a worthwhile investment. Not only do boys and girls from public schools enjoy a certain prestige later in life, but the public schools are often able, by offering status and fringe benefits, to attract higher-qualified staff. Classes in public schools are usually smaller than those in state schools so that pupils receive more individual attention.

The exclusive nature of the public schools has received much criticism in recent years. A number of committees have been set up to consider ways in which the independent schools could be incorporated into the state system but their recommendations have not been acted upon. In 1944 the Fleming Committee suggested that public schools should offer at least 25 per cent of their places to pupils from state primary schools. The Newsom Committee, set up in 1965 by the Labour Government to consider how the public schools could be best integrated with the state system, recommended that up to 50 per cent of the places at boarding schools should be made generally available. After the defeat of Labour in 1970 the Newsom Committee was disbanded and its proposals shelved. It seems unlikely that the public schools will ever be closed by parliamentary legislation, and the return of the Conservative Government in 1979 indicated that any immediate danger of closure was past. Indeed, it is highly probable that the Conservative Government's policy of introducing spending cuts, with its inevitable effect on state schools, has encouraged parents who can afford it to send their children to public school.

THE EXAMINATION SYSTEM

It is intended to replace the existing General Certificate of Education Ordinary Level and the Certificate of Secondary Education examinations in England and Wales with a new General Certificate of Secondary Education (GCSE). Like the examinations it replaces the GCSE will be taken at 16. Courses for the new certificate started in autumn 1986 and the first examinations will take place two years later, in the summer of 1988. The introduction of the new examination has been the cause of a considerable amount of controversy as many teachers and educationalists (not to mention parents) consider that the Government has allocated insufficient funds to finance teacher training and capital expenditure, while there is also a considerable body of opinion that believes the new system has been introduced too quickly. At one time it seemed that the teachers would refuse to co-operate with the education authorities over the timetable for the new examination as they were taking industrial action over pay and conditions, but the dispute was settled in May 1986. For the time being the Advanced Level GCE examination will continue to serve as the school leaving examination for those who continue in full-time education after the age of 16, but discussions are taking place as to how this examination might be modified. Scotland has its own examination system, pupils take the Scottish Certificate of Education at the Ordinary Level at 16 and the 'Higher' at 18.

Higher Education

Broadly speaking, 'higher education' covers universities, polytechnics, colleges and institutes of higher education, together with Scottish central institutions. There are a total of 53 university institutions in Britain, 31 polytechnics, 14 Scottish central institutions and more than 450 colleges offering higher education qualifications, that is, degree courses or professional qualifications. During the academic year 1983–4 there were 301,000 full-time students in universities, 171,000 in polytechnics and central institutions, and a further 110,000 at other colleges. There were also 316,000 part-time students, giving a total student population of 897,000.

Perhaps the most significant influence on the development of higher education since the Second World War was the Robbins Committee, appointed in 1961 by the Macmillan Government to report on higher education needs. The committee, in its report published in 1964, recommended a significant expansion of higher education, so that all those requiring a place would be able to obtain one. The subsequent expansion of higher education in the 1960s was dramatic – many universities expanded their intake considerably, while a number of new institutions were established to complement those that already existed. Robbins had predicted that between the academic year 1962–3 and that of 1967–8 there would be a 51 per cent expansion of numbers in higher education, in fact the growth rate was 74 per cent. This expansion continued into the 1970s, but at a slower rate than the dramatic expansion of the 1960s, so that in the last academic year of the decade there were 265,000 UK students at universities and 202,000 attending other institutions. This slowing down has continued into the 1980s and for the first time there has been talk of universities having to close down. Up until the middle of the decade no university was forced to close its doors, but the New University of Colraine in Northern Ireland amalgamated with the Ulster Polytechnic and a number of colleges of the University of London have joined forces. In 1985 the Government published a paper entitled *The Development of Higher Education into the 1990s*, which although it declared support for 'the Robbins' principle' made it clear that the selection for higher education courses in the future would be made more rigorous. It has also been made clear that institutes of higher education cannot rely exclusively on government funding in the future, but will have to develop their own means of raising funds.

UNIVERSITIES
At the beginning of the nineteenth century there were seven universities in Britain, only two of which were in England. By the beginning of the twentieth century a further five had been founded, while between 1900 and the mid-1960s another thirty-four universities were granted charters.

The oldest universities in Britain are Oxford and Cambridge -- often referred to jointly as 'Oxbridge' – founded at the end of the twelfth century. Until the reign of Henry II it had been the custom for English scholars to study at universities on the Continent, particularly at the University of Paris. Henry's quarrel with his archbishop, Thomas à Becket, led to the expulsion of Englishmen studying in France and the refugees set up their own institution at Oxford. Later some members of the Oxford community moved to Cambridge. The first Oxford college, University College, was founded in about 1249; the first Cambridge one, Peterhouse, in 1284. No further universities were established in England until the nineteenth century, although four were founded in Scotland between 1411 and 1582, while in 1591 Queen Elizabeth I granted a charter to Trinity College, Dublin.

Both Oxford and Cambridge restricted their membership to members of the Anglican Church until the nineteenth century, with the results that at various times the Dissenters (Nonconformists) tried to set up their own higher education institutions. Although some of these had considerable success in the short term, they were unable to establish themselves as universities. It was not until the 1830s when the universities of Durham and London opened their doors that non-Anglicans were admitted to higher education.

During the second half of the nineteenth century a number of institutes for advanced education were set up, particularly in the north of England. Some of these, such as Owen's College in Manchester and the Yorkshire College at Leeds, were to develop into universities in their own right at the turn of the century. These universities, which include Manchester, Liverpool and Bristol, are often referred to as 'the civic universities', although they are more popularly known as 'redbrick universities', a name said to be derived from the colour of the building material of the University of Birmingham.

The second-generation civic universities include a number of institutions that started life as university colleges, that is university-level institutions which could not award their own degrees. Instead they prepared students for the 'external degrees' of the University of London. These institutions acquired full university status just before, or shortly after, the Second World War. Universities of this kind include Leicester, Hull and Nottingham.

In 1949 the University College of North Staffordshire (later the University of Keele) was founded. Although a university college, this institution awarded its own degrees from the start, as has been the case with all universities founded since 1949. The universities of the 1960s fall into two categories: in the first place there were the 'new' universities, completely new foundations, usually situated on the outskirts of provincial towns like Brighton (the University of Sussex) and York. Secondly, there were the former colleges of advanced technology, which formed the basis of technological universities, for example Loughborough, Bradford and Salford. Seven of the 'new' universities were set up in England, one in Scotland, and one in Ulster. England was also given seven technological universities, while two more were established in Scotland.

The last university that should be mentioned is the Open University (see p. 97), which accepted its first students in 1970.

British universities therefore have been founded at different times, in response to different needs. Thus there is little apparent similarity between the University of Oxford, founded in the thirteenth century mainly for the training of priests, and the University of Loughborough, founded in the 1960s, which is primarily concerned with producing technologists and engineers. Another reason for differences is that universities have always been planned and set up at the local level, even when the greater part of their funds has come from the state. Thus, even when a number of universities have been founded at the same time, their structures may differ considerably. For example,

York, Kent, Sussex and East Anglia were all established during the 1960s. The first two have a collegiate system, derived from the ancient universities; the other two have a structure that is more like that of the civil universities, although with many distinctive features. The type and content of courses may also differ a great deal from university to university, as may entrance requirements, staff–student ratios, teaching methods, and so on.

Nevertheless, in spite of the differences between the social and academic environments of the universities, there are certain features that they all have in common. In the first place there are no state universities in Britain, although the state provides some 90 per cent of the universities' expenditure through the University Grants Committee. In the early 1980s the University Grants Committee began to take a more intrusive role in deciding how the money it allocated should be spent and, after a series of visits to university-level institutions throughout the country, it wrote to the authorities of each telling them how much money they would be allowed. In a number of cases the grants were cut significantly and, as a result, some universities were forced to close down departments and make staff redundant. Because a large proportion of the staff at universities are employed on contracts that provide them with tenure – i.e. that is, they cannot be dismissed except for grave offences – the cost of 'buying out' staff was considerable.

Secondly, the standards for first degrees are intended to be the same at all universities, although in practice one university may have greater prestige than another. In England and Wales, studying for a first degree normally takes three years, except for subjects such as medicine and dentistry where courses are invariably longer. At the end of a first degree course, the successful student is awarded a Bachelor's degree, usually a Bachelor of Arts (BA) or Bachelor of Science (BSc). In Scotland the first degree is a Master's degree which is awarded after four years of study. In English and Welsh universities a Master's degree is awarded after a further period of study, except at Oxford and Cambridge where it is possible to purchase an MA twelve years after graduating as a BA. The names and standards of higher degrees vary between differing universities.

As far as the administration of universities is concerned there is a basic similarity between the various institutions, although details may differ. In England and Wales the nominal head of the university is the Chancellor, who is usually a distinguished public figure, often a member of the royal family or the aristocracy. The Chancellor appears at degree-giving ceremonies and on other appropriate occasions, but his or her duties are almost completely ceremonial and he or she takes no part in the day-to-day running of the university. The professional head of the university is the Vice-Chancellor, who in most cases is an academic of professorial rank. At most universities the Vice-Chancellorship is a permanent position, but at Oxford the office is held by heads of colleges for a period of three years.

The bodies and committees which run the administrative and academic side of the university vary from institution to institution. In some universities members of the academic staff and students have far more say than in others, while obviously the large collegiate University of London with some 22,000 students and 800 professors in about thirty schools, requires a totally different structure from that of a small provincial institution such as Keele, with less than 2,000 students and fewer than thirty professors. Nevertheless, there are certain features that are common to most universities and these are outlined below.

The University Court is usually a large body consisting of local dignitaries, such as Members of Parliament, local councillors, church leaders and others, together with members of the academic staff. However, in most cases the powers of the Court are purely formal. Executive control of the university is vested in the Council, composed of persons nominated by the Court, local authorities and senior academics. The Council is principally concerned with finance and seeing that the university is able to meet its responsibilities.

The Senate is the principal academic body of the university. It is responsible for academic policy, teaching, examinations and discipline. The Senate is usually made up mainly of senior academics, although there is a trend towards including more junior members of staff and, in some cases, students. Academic work is the responsibility of faculties, each of which is headed by a Dean. A faculty consists of a number of departments, and the head of department is usually a professor. Large departments will often have more than one professor, and may be subdivided according to the particular interests of the holders of the professorial chairs. The position of 'reader' is usually reserved for senior members of staff with strong research interests and, in some cases, a reader may in fact be the head of a small department. Senior lecturers and lecturers are responsible for much of the teaching provided by the department, but they are also expected to engage in research.

Most academic staff divide their time between teaching and research and, in the case of senior staff, they may often find that they have a considerable administrative load as well. Most university teaching, at least in the arts and social sciences, is done through lectures, supplemented by tutorials and seminars. The amount of individual attention given to students varies from one university to another. At Oxbridge great emphasis is put on the tutorial system, and students receive a considerable amount of personal tuition. At many provincial universities, however, the weekly tutorial, where students are taught in small groups, is not possible. The British universities have, with some justification, prided themselves on their favourable staff–student ratio, in the mid-1980s this was one staff member to every nine students.

The Open University   The Open University was granted its charter in 1969, and started to enrol its first students the following year. Originally the Open University was conceived as 'the university of the second chance', designed to provide degree-level courses for those who for one reason or another had been unable to take advantage of a conventional university education when they left school. There are no formal entrance requirements and recent advertisements for the university have emphasised that people from all occupations are eligible to become students. In spite of hopes that the university would achieve a significant break through in providing university education for people who were excluded from the conventional system, a large proportion of the first students were teachers seeking to improve their qualifications. Some people have gone as far as to say that the Open University is a failure because it has not reached the people for whom it was intended. On the other hand, the Open University on the eve of its first graduation day had nearly 40,000 students, which indicates that it is filling a need. In 1974 the university took its first 500 school-leavers.

There are no conventional lectures or classes. Students study in their own homes with the aid of lectures broadcast on television and radio supplemented by course material prepared by tutors. The Open University has thirteen regional directors, each responsible for providing support services for the students in his or her area. The regional director maintains contact with local organisations, such as libraries, and local education authorities, and with the headquarters of the Open University at Milton Keynes. He or she also runs local study centres and appoints local counsellors and course tutors. Counsellors are expected to help students with any educational problems they may encounter, while tutors hold courses for students in local study centres. Students are also expected to attend a summer school each year.

For the authorities one of the attractions of the Open University is that it is relatively cheap. It is estimated that the average recurrent cost per student at the Open University is a quarter of that for a conventional university, and as more students are enrolled so costs per student fall.

POLYTECHNICS

The Robbins Committee recommended that 'higher education' should be concentrated in the universities, while 'further education', non-degree level courses, should be given in local authority colleges and technical institutions. However, in 1966, the Labour Government announced that it intended to develop higher education outside the university sector, and designate a number of polytechnics. These polytechnics grdually came into being during the late 1960s and early 1970s. In most cases polytechnics were formed from institutions that already existed (for example, in some cities the college of technology, the college of commerce and the college of art were combined); in others, an entirely new institution was set up. Many colleges of education, designed for training teachers, are now incorporated in polytechnics. The amalgamations meant that many newly designated polytechnics found that they were expected to continue to operate in the buildings occupied by the constituent parts. In some areas polytechnics did get new buildings, although it is significant that these were for the most part much less lavish than those occupied by the new universities.

Polytechnics are financed and controlled by local authorities. The number of students taking degree courses differs from institution to institution; at some 90 per cent more of the students are reading for degrees, but elsewhere the figure is much lower. Some of the institutions designated as polytechnics have had degree-level courses for many years, but nearly all of these were the somewhat rigid London University external degrees. In 1964 the Council for National Academic Awards (CNAA) was established, and today a large number of polytechnic students are working for CNAA degrees. Under the CNAA scheme polytechnics draw up their own courses which are then submitted to the appropriate CNAA board for approval. In order for a course to be accepted the polytechnic must convince the board that the standard of lecturers teaching the course and the facilities that the polytechnic can offer, in terms of library size or laboratories, are satisfactory.

STUDENTS
Students taking full-time degree courses at universities, colleges of education and polytechnics are entitled to study grants from local education authorities. At the end of December 1985 it was announced that student grants would go up by 2 per cent in 1986, which means that a student studying outside London gets £1,866 a year, while one studying in London, where costs are higher gets £2,207. However, only about three students in ten get the full grant as parents' incomes are taken into account when grants are allocated. In 1985 the National Union of Students (NUS) estimated that parents pay £230 million in grants, while the state pays £527 million. The amount received by students is worked out according to a sliding scale, but it is estimated that over 40 per cent of parents do not make up the grant to the recommended figure.

Students at British universities tend to be younger than those at many similar institutions on the Continent. One reason for this is probably the fact that because the majority of courses only last for three years, and this is the period for which the grant is paid, students spend a relatively short time on their studies. The majority of British students go to university straight from school at the age of 18, which means that they have completed their studies by the time they are 21 or 22. As there is no military service, boys as well as girls are able to continue their studies from sixth form to a higher education without a break. Many of the students at polytechnics are older than those at universities, as they may well have served in industry or commerce for some years before coming to take a degree. Indeed, many courses at polytechnics are 'sandwich courses', where engineers or trainee managers will work for a qualification at the same time as doing a job. A relatively small number of students are married. This is partly due to the fact that most students are quite young and also because, until recently, if two students married the wife's grant was greatly reduced. Many students therefore preferred to live together without getting married, and receive two full grants, rather than exist in 'respectable' poverty on a much smaller amount. In 1975 the regulations were changed, although not as radically as the NUS had hoped.

Facilities for students vary greatly between universities. The standard of accommodation at some Oxbridge colleges is very high indeed; students have well-appointed rooms and servants provided by the college. At the other end of the scale, students are expected to compete for flats and bed-sitters on the open market. Most of the new universities try to provide student hostels or halls of residence, and a number of the older institutions have also been building these whenever possible. In general the amenities enjoyed by university students are superior to those for polytechnic students.

Students wishing to attend a university in England must first apply to the Universities Central Council on Admissions (UCCA), giving details of their qualifications, or expected qualifications, and the course they wish to follow. They also list the universities of their choice in order of preference. The Council then forwards the applications to the universities who make the decision whether to accept or reject the candidate. Students wishing to study at a polytechnic apply direct.

Further Education

Further education is provided by institutes of higher education, colleges of further education and technical colleges, which are financed and administered by local authorities. These colleges provide a wide range of technical and vocational training, to full-time or part-time students. Many full-time students are studying for GCE examinations, perhaps with the intention of going on to take a degree, though others are taking courses that will qualify them for a particular career. In many colleges of technology and institutes of higher education CNAA-validated degree courses are also provided. A large number of the students at technical colleges are taking day-release courses – in other words they are working in a factory or workshop for four days a week and attending the college on the other day – or block release courses, which means that they attend full-time for a period of two months or so.

There are a wide range of adult education and 'extra-mural' classes available throughout the country, run by extra-mural departments of the universities, the Workers' Educational Association and local education authorities. Subjects covered include languages, local history, archaeology, painting, judo, cookery, pottery, photography and a host of others.

7

The Industrial State

During the Middle Ages, Britain, like the rest of Europe, was a rural country. Most of the population lived in villages or small country settlements and depended on agriculture for the necessities of life. The sixteenth and seventeenth centuries brought important developments in political and economic life, but as technological advances did not keep pace with these the pattern of life did not change a great deal. It was not until the beginning of the eighteenth century that technological developments began to catch up with changes in the political and economic system; once they did, however, the effect was dramatic. Inventions such as those by Newcomen, Watt, Darby and Kay were to change Britain, in a relatively short period of time, from a rural nation dependent on agriculture to an urban one growing rich on the power of the machine.

Towards the end of the seventeenth century a number of financial institutions began to develop in England, the most important being the Bank of England, founded in 1694. The existence of a comparatively sophisticated financial structure through which credit could be obtained did a great deal to encourage the development of trade and industry during the next century. Other important factors included a plentiful supply of raw materials, such as coal and iron ore, and Britain's trading position astride the sea routes to the New World.

By the early years of the nineteenth century Britain had won a commanding lead over the rest of the world as far as industrialisation was concerned and proceeded to exploit her position. Her dominance of world trade was to be of relatively short duration and by the end of the 1870s it was virtually over. Nevertheless, in spite of increasing competition Britain managed to retain her lead in a number of fields, while the City of London continued to be the centre of world trade well into the twentieth century.

At the end of the nineteenth century Britain's main rivals in the

101

struggle for economic leadership were Germany, united under the leadership of Bismarck after the Franco-Prussian War, and the USA, which was fast developing its industrial potential. Before the end of the century both these countries had overtaken the United Kingdom in the production of steel. By 1900 the USA was making twice as much steel as the UK (USA 10·1 million tons, Germany 6·2 million tons, UK 4·9 million tons). The First World War and the economic difficulties of the interwar years caused many problems for Britain, although in 1938 she still accounted for about 22 per cent of the world's exports of manufactured goods. This figure has been declining since the Second World War as international competition has grown more intense, and by the mid-1980s was no more than 5 per cent.

One of Britain's major problems in the period since the Second World War is that her balance of payments situation has been far from satisfactory, although in practice the strength of 'invisible exports', such as financial services provided by the City of London, shipping and aviation services, and tourism have kept the current account in the black. Another factor that has had a favourable effect on the balance of payments is the contribution made by North Sea oil since the mid-1970s. However, it is clear that the reserves of oil in the waters immediately adjacent to Britain are finite and there will undoubtedly be grave problems when Britain changes from being the sixth largest producer of crude oil in the world, as she was in the mid-1980s, to being an importer again.

In the postwar period successive governments have tried to come to terms with Britain's economic difficulties through a variety of measures. (Labour Governments have tended to favour direct intervention in economic planning, nationalising key industries and laying down strict guidelines for the conduct of trade and commerce, while Conservative Governments have tended to permit a greater degree of freedom.) However, Governments of both political persuasions have had trouble maintaining the value of the currency. The Labour Government devalued in 1949 and again in 1967, while in June 1972 the Heath government allowed the pound to float. The Conservative Government that took office in May 1979 was faced with soaring inflation and unemployment running at over a million. It believed that the key problem of the British economy was inflation, and it hoped that by reducing this it would increase Britain's competitiveness in world trade, and to achieve this it adopted a policy of minimum intervention. The results of the Conservative policy have hardly been more successful than those of previous Governments – the trade balance has swung from deficit to credit and back again, the pound rose in value against the dollar to a rate of £1 = $2·35 and then sank down to near parity (at the beginning of 1986 it stood at £1 = $1.40), while unemployment has risen to over 3 million.

In the mid-1970s manufactured and semi-manufactured goods accounted for 80 per cent of the country's exports. Ten years later this figure was down to 66 per cent. Engineering products, including industrial machinery, motor vehicles, electrical equipment, aerospace products, ships and agricultural machinery remain the largest single group of export products, but their share has declined at the expense of chemicals, food and drink, and various services. In fact in 1983 it was estimated that overseas earnings from services amounted to almost half the value of exports from manufactures, the value of manufactured goods being £45,000 million and the value of services £20,000 million. Britain's most important trading partners are the countries of the European Economic Community – Britain became a full member in 1973 – the USA, Japan, Sweden and Switzerland.

The British Economy Today

During the nineteenth century the policy of both Liberal and Conservative Governments was to interfere as little as possible in the commercial life of the country. The general belief was that trade was best left in the hands of the businessman. This *laissez-faire* attitude might have been acceptable when Britain dominated world trade, but increasing competition in international markets, to say nothing of the complexity of managing the domestic economy, have meant that twentieth-century governments have had to take a much greater part in economic planning.

Government participation in economic decision-making has increased to such an extent over the years that in the 1950s a Conservative minister was moved to say, 'We are all planners now'. His comment at the time was apt for, even though the Conservatives held the view that the economy should operate with the minimum of government intervention, until the late 1970s the Conservatives were actively involved in detailed planning which, although inspired by different political motives than the Labour Party, sought to control economic conditions. Broadly speaking the Conservative Party believes in the 'profit motive' and the enhancement of the individual's position through his or her own endeavours, while the Labour Party believes that the economy should be managed for the benefit of society as a whole. As a means to this end, the Labour Party's policy is that certain key industries should be under the control of the state, and industries in this category at the present time include coal, steel, the railways, ship-building, aerospace and the public utilities. When the Conservatives returned to power in 1979 they announced that they were intending to loosen the constraints that had been imposed by previous Conservative and Labour administrations and permit greater competitiveness. By allowing 'market forces' to be the ultimate controller of the survival or demise of industry they claimed that the British economy would expand more quickly and on a firmer base than had been possible in the past. As we have seen, the key planks in the Conservative programme were to reduce inflation, increase competitiveness, and encourage the expansion of industry through encouraging investment and removing restrictions on entrepreneurs. Certainly the Thatcher government's record on inflation seems to have shown some success – down from 14 per cent in 1979 to 3 per cent in 1986, but unemployment has soared from 5·1 per cent in 1979 to 13·1 per cent in 1986. Matters were not helped by the fact that the early 1980s saw a world recession of major proportions, but it is also true to say that when the world economy did start to recover, Britain's recovery started later and proceeded more slowly than that in other industrial countries, particularly her major competitors in Western Europe and the USA.

CONTROL OF INDUSTRY

State Ownership   Up until 1945 nationalisation had been on a relatively small scale, but the Labour Government that came to power in that year was committed to a comprehensive nationalisation programme. In 1946 the Bank of England was taken over by the state, to be followed in the same year by the coalmines and civil aviation. The Transport Act of 1947 nationalised the railways, canals and some road transport, while in 1948 and 1949 gas and iron and steel were added to the list (electricity had been nationalised in 1926). The Conservatives denationalised iron and steel in 1953, but the industry was taken over again by the Labour Government in 1967. The Labour Party does not have a monopoly of nationalisation, however, for in 1954 the Conservatives set up the

United Kingdom Atomic Energy Authority to develop nuclear power for peaceful purposes. In 1971 another Conservative Government nationalised Rolls-Royce after financial difficulties drove the company into liquidation.

It can scarcely be said that the nationalised industries have had an easy history. The establishment of the public sector and its role has produced a great deal of discussion in Parliament, in board rooms throughout the country and in a large number of other places. One of the issues that has caused most argument is how the public industries should be run. The fundamental question here is whether they should be expected to make a profit or whether they should be operated primarily as a public service, being subsidised when necessary by the government. This problem is well illustrated by the railways. When the railways were nationalised by the Transport Act of 1947 they had been making a loss for a number of years. Public ownership did not change the situation, and the question of profit versus public service was soon being hotly debated. The Act nationalising the railways had said that they should pay their way but a large labour force (648,740 workers in 1948), outdated equipment and a large number of uneconomic branch lines made this difficult to achieve. In 1963, however, the then chairman of British Railways, Dr Richard Beeching, published his rationalisation plan, which recommended that track mileage should be cut from 17,000 to 8,000 and that 70,000 jobs should be phased out. The report produced an immediate outcry from the public, who stood to lose their rail services, and from the railway unions, whose members were threatened with redundancy. A long and bitter discussion ensued as to whether Beeching's proposals should be implemented. On commercial grounds his findings made a great deal of sense. The railways had been planned for the needs of the nineteenth century, before road transport had developed on any scale. Fierce competition between rival companies meant that in some cases main lines duplicated each other, while country lines had lost much of their traffic to other forms of transport, particularly the family car. Nevertheless, there were large numbers of people who did not have cars and for whom withdrawal of services would cause hardship, and it was for this reason that Beeching's critics argued that social costs should also be taken into consideration when planning future rail services, as the railways were owned by the state. Taking social costs into account would, of course, mean that financial subsidies would have to be provided. In the event, many of Beeching's proposals were adopted; but British Rail continued to lose money.

The Conservative government elected in 1979 announced that it intended to privatise many of the nationalised industries and since the election it has sold a number of companies including British Aerospace, Cable & Wireless, the National Freight Consortium, Britoil, and British Telecom, while plans exist to transfer other state-controlled corporations to private ownership. The sale of all these organisations has caused a great deal of political debate in the country; critics of the policy have claimed that shares were sold too cheaply, while the Labour Party has warned that once it is returned to power it will reintroduce nationalisation in key areas.

Private Enterprise　While control of the industries in the public sector is ultimately in the hands of Parliament, in the private sector, control is vested in those who have a financial interest in a particular company. In most private companies ownership is concentrated in a few hands, and in practice the directors of a large number of small businesses are members of the same family. Expansion inevitably requires capital and, in the first instance, this often means a loan from a bank or similar institution. Really large-scale developments, however, are frequently financed by 'going public', which means that members of the public are given a chance to invest money in the company and thus participate in its fortunes. Money is invested by buying stocks or shares on the Stock Exchange. Stocks are loans, either to the government (gilt-edged) or to companies, which earn a fixed-interest return. Shares, however, mean that the purchaser actually becomes an owner of the company in which he or she is investing money, although this ownership may well be shared with several thousand other people. The shareholders as owners of the company are responsible for appointing the board of directors, who run the company on their behalf. In practice the majority of shareholders are more interested in receiving their dividend than in interfering with how the company is run, and so most boards of directors tend to be self-perpetuating.

In recent years there has been a trend towards amalgamations between companies. For some years after the Second World War the pattern was one of large companies buying up their smaller competitors, but although this still continues there has been since the 1960s a tendency towards mergers between groups of comparable size. Such mergers could be seen in all sections of industry: electronics, communications, motor vehicles and the food and service industries. It is estimated that in 1981 the 100 largest companies accounted for 34 per cent of manufacturing employment. The largest manufacturing companies in the United Kingdom in 1983 were: BAT industries – with interests in tobacco, food, insurance and paper; Imperial Chemical Industries – whose interests included chemicals, man-made fibres and minerals; Unilever – food and consumer items; General Electric Company – electronics and associated products; Imperial Group – tobacco, food, and so on; Ford Motor Company (US-controlled) – motor vehicles and engines; British Leyland – motor vehicles; Rothmans (South African-controlled) – tobacco, food; George Weston – food and services; Associated British Foods – food and services. It is significant how many of the largest UK companies are in the food and service industries, and it is true to say that these are the sectors that have seen the most significant expansion of their market share in recent years – at the expense of manufacturing industries.

The concentration of economic power in fewer hands, brought about by the mergers of the 1960s, concerned the Government of the day and in 1965 the powers of the then Board of Trade (now part of an enlarged Department of Trade and Industry) to investigate mergers were increased. In 1965 the Monopolies and Mergers Act strengthened the Monopolies Commission that had been established in 1948, and Government powers in this area were further strengthened in 1973 by the Fair Trading Act, which is administered by the Director of Fair Trading. In 1976 the Restrictive Trade Practices Act and the Resale Prices Acts were passed to control activities which were felt to be against the public interest. The Director General of Fair Trading can also investigate business practices that restrict competition under the terms of the Competition Act of 1980.

THE CITY
The City is roughly a square mile of banking houses, insurance firms and stockbrokers' offices, rubbing shoulders with such famous buildings as St Paul's Cathedral and the Tower of London. Although no longer the axis around which world trade revolves, London is still a financial centre of considerable importance. It is the largest international insurance market in the world, has important markets for the supply of goods and services, such as the Baltic Exchange and the London Metal Exchange, and is also the centre of the Sterling Area.

The financial power of the City originated centuries ago. During the Middle Ages merchants from London pioneered the wool trade with the Continent. In Tudor times the City invested in the voyages of explorers and privateers such as Sir Francis Drake, while the support of the City for the parliamentary cause was one of the reasons for the defeat of Charles I in the Civil War. Many of the great institutions of the City were first established during the seventeenth century. In the 1680s Edward Lloyd's coffee house, from which grew the great insurance firm of Lloyd's, began its operations, while in the last decade of the century the Bank of England was founded.

The Bank of England   The Bank of England was founded in 1694. It is interesting to note that, although it became banker to the government and the leading bank of issue, it was not until 1946 that the Bank was nationalised. It is no doubt due to this long period of independence that the Bank still operates with a certain amount of autonomy. Indeed, at times some MPs, particularly Labour MPs, have complained that the Bank has too much freedom of action and should be controlled more closely.

The Bank of England plays a very important role in the commercial life of the United Kingdom. In addition to acting as banker to the government, it is also banker for overseas central banks and commercial banks in Britain. In England and Wales all bank notes are issued by the Bank of England, although in Scotland and Northern Ireland a number of banks have this right. The Bank is also the manager of the Exchange Equalisation Account, which consists of gold and foreign currency. By use of this, the Bank can give support to the pound sterling in adverse market conditions. If, for example, there is large-scale conversion of pounds into German marks, the Bank can supply marks from the account and take sterling in exchange.

In addition to the responsibilities outlined above, the Bank also acts as a middleman between the commercial institutions of the City and the government. It advises the government on monetary matters, and is also expected to ensure that the measures adopted by the government are put into effect. Methods employed by the Bank for implementing government policy include the regulation of interest rates and the buying and selling of Treasury bills. The head of the Bank is the Governor, a government appointee, and he presides over a board of directors, also chosen by the government.

Other Banks   The most important clearing banks are the 'Big Four' – Midland, Barclays, National Westminster and Lloyds – branches or associates of which can be found in virtually every High Street in

Britain. The clearing banks between them provide the bulk of the banking services required by the British people: current and deposit accounts, short-term loans and advice on financial matters. The banks are closely involved in many aspects of national and international finance and some of the banking groups also have extensive overseas interests.

Other Financial Institutions   The merchant banks play an important role in London's activities as a commercial centre. Although there are some sixty concerns which could be described as merchant banks, the most exclusive are the seventeen which belong to the Accepting Houses Committee. The merchant banks are involved in a wide range of activities. Some specialise, while others are active in a number of different fields. Broadly speaking, their sphere of operations lies in one or more of the following areas: they manage funds for individuals and trusts; they finance foreign trade; they advise industrial companies (there are few major takeovers that get very far before both sides call in a merchant bank); and they are involved in the foreign security business, providing an important link between London and overseas banking centres. During the last few years, a number of foreign banks, particularly banks based in the USA, have taken an interest in London merchant banks, and this trend is likely to continue now that new regulations covering the Stock Exchange and other financial institutions have come into effect during the second half of 1986.

The Stock Exchange was formally established in London in 1802. During the nineteenth century other stock markets were developed in provincial centres, but at the end of the century they were tending to amalgamate. In 1967 the provincial exchanges grouped themselves into six regional exchanges, while in 1973 the seven exchanges in the British Isles – London, Glasgow, Dublin, Manchester, Belfast, Liverpool and Birmingham – amalgamated as the Stock Exchange of Great Britain and Ireland. On 1 March 1986 new legislation governing membership of the Stock Exchange came into force. Under the new regulations membership of the Exchange was made available to Corporate Firms or Individual Members. There are strict rules governing the entrance of Members into the Stock Exchange and the conduct of business once they have been admitted. Members of the Stock Exchange buy and sell securities in both the international and domestic market, deal in 'gilts', bonds, options and financial futures. In 1980 the Unlisted Securities Market (USM) was established to deal in the securities of small companies, who did not wish to obtain a Stock Exchange listing.

Lloyd's is probably best known for its world-wide involvement in maritime insurance. Although this still produces a large amount of revenue, Lloyd's also has interests in many other fields. It is said that it is possible to insure against anything provided the price is right, and Lloyd's goes a long way towards proving this by providing insurance for statesmen against assassination or serious injury, for farmers against hurricanes and for shipping and air firms against loss of their ships or aircraft, or injury to their passengers. Lloyd's is not a company, but a market for insurance, where individual underwriters transact business. To become an underwriting member of Lloyd's rigorous financial requirements have to be satisfied, designed to ensure complete business integrity. While Lloyd's is the best-known insurance institution there are nearly 850 insurance companies in the United Kingdom handling both international and national business. British companies handle about 20 per cent of general insurance placed on the international market, while London is the world centre for reinsurance.

In recent years there have been a number of scandals in the City that have caused anxiety among many people and, as a result, a number of steps have been taken to introduce new measures of regulations. One of the most significant of these is the setting up of a Securities and Investment Board, which among other things will have the power to require self-regulating organisations – such as the Stock Exchange – to amend rules if it is thought that they do not offer sufficient protection for investors. The full powers of the Securities and Investment Board is laid down by the Financial Services Bill introduced in 1986.

Industrial Relations

TRADE UNIONS

Although the origins of the trade union movement are often traced back to the craft guilds of the Middle Ages, the modern trade union is essentially a product of the Industrial Revolution. During the late eighteenth century there were a number of attempts by workers to improve their conditions, and these were usually resisted by the authorities. In 1799 and 1800 Parliament, fearful that the events of the French Revolution might be repeated in Britain, passed the Combination Laws. These Laws, by forbidding working men the right to combine to negotiate for better wages and conditions, effectively checked the growth of unions until 1824, when they were repealed. In 1825, however, a new Act was passed, which once again restricted the right of men to take effective industrial action. During the late 1920s and early 1930s a number of unions were formed, but were subject to continual harassment.

By the 1840s a number of unions were in existence, usually drawing their membership from those who practised a particular craft. In addition to bargaining with employers these unions were particularly concerned with providing sickness grants and similar benefits for their members. They were still restricted by anti-union legislation, but the first trades union congress which met in 1868 could claim to represent about 118,000 workers. During the next few decades the position of the trade unionist improved, although there were still many battles to be won. In 1900 there were rather more than 2 million workers who were members of 1,323 trade unions. Seventy years later the number of unionists had grown to about 11 million, although as a result of amalgamations the number of unions had fallen to about 480. It is estimated that over 75 per cent of trade unionists belong to the twenty-three largest unions. In spite of the tendency towards larger unions, a large number of British unions are still basically 'craft unions', that is, members belong to a union because they have a particular skill, rather than because they belong to a particular industry. This tends to keep the number of unions relatively large, and can also cause demarcation, or 'who does what', disputes. Britain has a labour force of over 26 million, nearly 12 million of whom belong to trade unions.

The central body of the British trade union movement is the Trades Union Congress (TUC). The Congress itself only meets once a year, when delegates from the member unions meet to discuss matters of concern to the movement. Each year this annual conference elects a General Council, consisting of thirty-four general secretaries of trade unions, and this Council acts as the voice of the TUC for the rest of the year. The only full-time member of the General Council is the General Secretary, who is also the chief officer of the TUC.

There are some 102 trade unions affiliated to the TUC – fewer than a decade ago largely due to amalgamations that have taken place in recent years – representing about 10·5 million unionists. It is estimated that almost 80 per cent of trade unionists belong to the twenty-five largest unions. The biggest unions are the Transport and General Workers Union, with over 1·5 million members, the Amalgamated

Union of Engineering Workers, and the General, Municipal, Boiler-makers and Allied Trades Union, both of which have about 1 million members.

Since the Second World War British industry has acquired a reputation for being strike-prone, although in fact the figure for days lost during the 1960s through industrial action – 5·4 million – compares favourably with other industrialised countries. In the 1970s the figure rose significantly, but even so the figure of 13 million days lost between 1971–80 gave Britain a better record than Canada, Italy and the USA. During the 1980s the number has declined again, and in 1983 stood at 3·8 million days lost through strikes. The reason for this reduction can probably be found in the considerable increase in unemployment in the 1980s.

In 1965 the Labour Government appointed a Royal Commission to study the trade union movement and this body reported in 1968. One of the key recommendations of the Royal Commission was that a Commission on Industrial Relations should be set up. This recommendation was put into effect, but as the Commission's role was to bring unions and employers together on a voluntary basis its powers were somewhat limited. Meanwhile, the Labour Government was working on a far more controversial measure, details of which were contained in a policy document entitled *In Place of Strife* published early in 1969. The proposals guaranteed the rights of unionists, but also contained measures that the trade unions regarded as totally unacceptable. After a long and bitter struggle within the Labour movement, the TUC announced that it was prepared to give a 'solemn and binding undertaking' to intervene in strikes where unionists were at fault. Although this voluntary declaration fell far short of what the Government was aiming at, the hostility of the unions forced it to back down, and shelve plans for legislation. The Conservative Party, which returned to power in 1970, had no such inhibitions. Shortly after the election the outline of an Industrial Relations Bill was drawn up, and this became law in August 1971. Under the Act, unions were required to register with the Registrar of Trade Unions and Employers' Associations. The Act also put the Commission on Industrial Relations on a statutory basis, set up the National Industrial Relations Court, and forbade 'unfair industrial practices' by employers and employees. The TUC felt that the Act restricted its rights and instructed member unions not to register. If a union did not register it would not, of course, be recognised as official, but the TUC obviously hoped that by adopting a policy of non-cooperation it could render the Act unworkable.

The Act came into effect at the beginning of 1972 and from then until its repeal by a Labour Government in mid-1974 it was a thorn in the flesh of labour relations in Britain. During 1974 the Labour Government announced that it and the unions had agreed that the future of labour relations in Britain would be decided within the terms of a 'social contract' (see p. 129). However, this well-meaning but extremely vague declaration of principle had little effect in a time of unprecedented inflation and economic despondency. In mid-1975 the Government announced that no pay increases were to exceed £6 a week. In September of that year, at the TUC's annual conference, the trade unions agreed to support the Government's plan by a two to one majority.

The Employment Protection Act of 1975, and the Trade Union and Labour Relations (Amendment) Act of the following year gave workers greater protection against dismissal, the right to higher redundancy payments and provided legal immunities for the unions. Unions were also given access to company information which was relevant to wage negotiations.

When the Conservatives returned to power in 1979 they introduced the Employment Acts of 1980 and 1982 and the Trade Union Act of 1984 which restricted the powers of trade union officials by introducing secret ballots on issues such as official strikes, election of certain officials and the payment of levies to political parties. The Acts also introduced changes to the legal standing of trade unions, allowing them to be sued in the civil courts in certain circumstances, and established new regulations for picketing. Although the Government claimed that the Acts were designed to increase democracy in the trade union movement they were widely seen as an attack on the unity of the trade union movement. It is interesting to note that the requirement that unions had to take a secret ballot on the issue of a political levy backfired on the Conservatives, as the overwhelming majority of unions have voted in favour of a levy being paid to the Labour Party.

It is clear that the antagonism between the Thatcher Government and the TUC has increased since the 1979 election. This is partly due to the legislation outlined above; partly to the fact that the Government has rarely consulted the trade union movement on policy – as compared with the Labour Government which regularly sought the opinion of leading unionists – and partly to the anti-union stance adopted by

Conservative ministers to trade unionists in the civil service and the public sector. In 1984, for example, it was announced that civil servants working in a secret government establishment were no longer permitted to be members of a trade union, while between March 1984 and March 1985 the country experienced a miners' strike against government policy towards pit closures.

THE CONFEDERATION OF BRITISH INDUSTRY
The Confederation of British Industry (CBI) represents some 300,000 companies and acts as a mouthpiece for business. Matters of policy are decided by the 400-member Council and there is also a permanent staff headed by a director-general.

It provides advisory services to its members and represents the employers in any meetings between the trade unions, management and the government. In addition it maintains links with similar bodies in other countries.

THE ADVISORY, CONCILIATION AND ARBITRATION SERVICE
The Advisory, Conciliation and Arbitration Service (ACAS) was established in 1974. It is an independent body, although it is government-financed, and is designed to intervene in labour disputes at the request of the parties concerned. The board of ACAS consists of a chairman and nine other members and has the power to nominate an arbitrator (frequently a leading academic with industrial relations experience) if it feels that such a course is appropriate.

8

Life in
Britain Today

Population

At the beginning of the nineteenth century most of the inhabitants of the United Kingdom lived in the country. According to the first official census in 1801, the population of England and Wales was 8·8 million, 7·3 million of whom lived in the countryside. In 1831 agriculture still accounted for the largest sector of the country's labour force, giving work to 28 per cent of all families. By 1851 the population had risen to nearly 18 million, half of them living in urban areas, London, which had grown in size from just over 1 million in 1801 to 2·6 million in 1851, was by far the largest city, but industrial centres such as Liverpool, Manchester and Birmingham had also expanded at an unprecedented rate. In 1801 Birmingham had 71,000 inhabitants; fifty years later there were 233,000 people living in the city, while Manchester had grown from 75,000 to 303,000 and Liverpool from 82,000 to 376,000. By the middle of the twentieth century London's population was 8·3 million and Birmingham's 1·1 million, while Manchester and Liverpool had 703,000 and 789,000 inhabitants respectively. It seems that 1951 represented the peak population in the large cities, for at the time of the 1961 census London had 8·1 million inhabitants, while other large cities showed similar small, but none the less significant, falls in population.

At the time of the 1981 census the population of the United Kingdom was 53,556,911 living at a density of 231 per square kilometre. In common with other industrialised countries, Britain has experienced a fall in both birth and death rates during the twentieth century. This has meant that although fewer people have been born, they are surviving longer. In 1870 the birth rate was 35·5 per 1,000 and the death rate 22·9 per 1,000; in 1983 the figures for England and Wales were 12·7

115

per 1,000 and 11·7 per 1,000 respectively. At the beginning of the 1870s the average expectation of life was 41 years for men and 45 years for women; in 1984 it was 70 for men and 76 for women. Lack of effective methods of birth control, among other factors, meant that the average nineteenth-century family consisted of between five and six children. Many children, however, did not reach maturity, succumbing to diseases that have virtually disappeared in the twentieth century. In 1870 the infant mortality rate in the United Kingdom was 150 per 1,000; at the beginning of the 1980s it was 11·1 per 1,000.

Marriage and Family Life

Although marriage remains a popular institution in Britain – 64 per cent of the population over 16 are married – there have been considerable changes in the pattern of relationships in recent years. In 1972 there were nearly half a million marriages in the United Kingdom; by 1981 the number had declined to under 400,000 and there has also been an increase in the average age for first marriages. At the same time, the number of marriages ending in divorce has increased from 2 in every 1,000 married couples in 1961 to 12 in every 1,000 in 1981. (These figures are for England and Wales – rates for Scotland and Northern Ireland are lower, reflecting the different religious and cultural structure of these parts of the United Kingdom.) The rise in the divorce rate in recent years has been seen by some as evidence of declining moral standards, but it is probably more realistic to account for it by changes in the law and social attitudes. In 1969 the Divorce Reform Act was passed which states that the only ground for divorce is that the marriage has 'irretrievably broken down'. This means that while adultery, cruelty and desertion, previously regarded as grounds for divorce, could be (and are) still used as evidence that a marriage has broken down, the committing of such acts is no longer the only cause of divorce. An important new provision in the Act was that a divorce can be granted, after two years' separation, if a couple agree that they want their marriage terminated. It is also possible for a marriage to be brought to an end on the petition of one spouse after a period of five years' separation. In 1984 a new Act was passed which put a time limit on the amount of time that a divorced spouse could receive maintenance. This Act was criticised by many women's organisations which felt that it discriminated against women as they usually suffered most financially when a marriage broke up.

With increasing urbanisation, old family patterns have been broken down. When people lived in one community for most of their lives they tended to remain in close contact with members of the family. Many farms, for example, were worked on a family basis, which meant that a man would meet his parents, brothers and sisters virtually every day. Other businesses, notably small shops and service trades, were also often run by families, and even today one still comes across evidence of this in the names of firms: for example W. H. Grant & Sons Ltd, Williams Bros (Brothers). Today, however, many families have their members scattered throughout the country, and meetings are irregular, usually taking place on special occasions such as weddings or funerals. Nevertheless, a large number of families still maintain regular contact, which is easier today than it used to be as a result of improved communications. Many parents keep in touch with their married or unmarried children by telephone, while widespread car ownership means that relations can be visited at weekends and during holidays. Although most young couples would undoubtedly like to set up their own homes, this is often financially impossible, so many spend the first year or so of their married life living with one or other set of parents. The problem of old people is also one that is often solved within the family context. A feature of late twentieth century Britain is that the age structure of the country is changing. With a falling birth rate – 694,000 live births in England, Scotland and Wales in 1983; 2,000 fewer than 1982 – there has been a decline in the proportion of people under 16 and an increase in the proportion of elderly people, especially those over the age of 85. Some 18 per cent were over retirement age (60 for women, 65 for men) compared with 15 per cent in 1961. In 1986, following a judgement in the European Court of Justice it was announced that legislation would be introduced giving women the legal right to work until the age of 65.

The Position of Women

Changes in family life are linked to changes in the position and role of women in British society. It is sometimes suggested that the position of women in nineteenth-century society can be summed up by the clothes they were expected to wear. The long hooped crinoline was no doubt extremely effective in concealing what was referred to in the phrase of the time as an 'interesting condition', but it had few other practical benefits. As far as upper- and middle-class women were concerned, their aim in life was to look after a man's home and to raise his family. Legally a wife's position was inferior to that of her husband, and most women were prepared to accept this status. It is ironical that although during the greater part of the nineteenth century there was a woman on the throne of Britain, members of her sex were not permitted to vote, take degrees at the ancient universities or, if married, own property in their own right. According to the law which prevailed during much of the nineteenth century, a woman's property passed to her husband on marriage, while any property she subsequently acquired also became his. Between 1870 and 1893 a number of Acts were passed to alter this situation and to establish the right of a married woman to retain her property.

It is interesting to note that even among the wealthy classes of society the education of girls was generally thought to be unnecessary. As far as most parents were concerned, girls were expected to be able to play a musical instrument, sew and conduct genteel conversation. Among the lower classes, education was likewise considered unnecessary, as most girls would find work as domestic servants, or in mills and factories. However, attitudes gradually changed as the century progressed and a number of schools for girls were founded. Bedford College, later to be a women's college of the University of London, was established in 1849, and Girton College, Cambridge in 1869 (although women were not granted Cambridge degrees until 1920). The 1870 Education Act provided elementary education for girls as well as boys. Increasing educational opportunities produced a desire for equal career opportunities and the right to vote. The first women's suffrage organisation was formed in the 1860s, although perhaps the best known was the Women's Social and Political Union founded by the Pankhursts in 1903. During the period leading up to the First World War the 'suffragettes' conducted a sustained campaign to win the vote for women. In 1918 they won their battle, although it is generally thought that the involvement of women in war work of various kinds did more for their cause than the demonstrations against the government. It is perhaps characteristic of the male politicians of 1918 that they could not resist adding a final insult to the women who were being enfranchised for the first time. Men had always been granted the vote at the age of 21; the 1918 Act gave the vote to women aged 30 and over, and it was not until the 1920s that they were given the vote on equal terms with men. In recent years women have been campaigning for greater equality in job opportunities and rates of pay (see also p. 127). The Sex Discrimination Act and the Equal Pay Act came into force in December 1975. The former made it unlawful for employers to discriminate between men and women when filling jobs (with a few exceptions), while the latter laid down that men and women doing the same job were entitled to similar rates of pay.

The Equal Opportunities Commission was set up in 1975 to enforce the Sex Discrimination and Equal Pay Acts. However, there are still quite considerable discrepancies between the payment received by men and women, partly because women tend to work part-time or work in jobs that only attract low wages. It is also clear that it is difficult for women to obtain promotion in both the public and private sectors and there are still relatively few women in top jobs in the civil service, industry, or education. In spite of the fact that Britain has had a female monarch, Queen Elizabeth II, since 1952, and has had a woman Prime Minister since 1979, the 42 per cent of women in the British workforce still have a long battle ahead to achieve equality.

Commonwealth Immigration

Another group who feel they have suffered considerably from discrimination in recent years are the Commonwealth immigrants. After the Second World War large numbers of people from the Commonwealth moved to Britain in order to find work and improved living conditions. Many of the newcomers came from 'new' Commonwealth countries, such as India, Pakistan and the West Indian islands. In 1962 the Conservative government introduced the Commonwealth Immigrants Act, which limited the number of people who were admitted to Britain each year. As the majority of immigrants were from the 'new' commonwealth and Pakistan the cry immediately went up that the Act was racialist in concept. These criticisms were redoubled when in 1968 and 1971 further Acts were passed which made entry even more difficult, especially for those with no ancestral ties with Britain.

It is estimated that there are about 1·5 million Commonwealth immigrants and families (many of whom have been born in the United Kingdom) in Britain, under 3 per cent of the total population. Many of the newcomers have tended to settle in towns in the Midlands and the north of England, while London also has a sizeable ethnic minority. In some areas there has been friction between the ethnic minorities and their white neighbours, and the situation has not been helped by the fact that a number of right-wing politicians have made speeches suggesting that repatriation schemes should be introduced. The Race Relations Act of 1976 makes discrimination on grounds of colour, race or ethnic or national origin unlawful. It also established the Commission for Racial Equality which replaced the Community Relations Commission that had been set up by the 1968 Race Relations Act

Sports and Entertainment

As we have seen, industrialisation and urbanisation had far-reaching effects on many aspects of life. Of particular importance is the effect of how people work, how they meet the challenge of new methods and new machines, and how they adapt to new pressures on their way of life. But they do not spend all their time working. They also take part in a variety of leisure-time activities; and in this area, as in others, there have been important changes in the last 150 years. When life was centred on the small rural community, amusements were for the most part provided by the villagers themselves. The most popular ways of relaxing seem to have been dancing and music-making, while a large number of games, legal and illegal, were also practised. On occasions these homemade amusements might be supplemented by travelling actors or musicians, or sometimes the country people might travel to a nearby town to see a boxing match, theatrical production, or similar entertainment. With the coming of the railways cheap travel became a reality; Thomas Cook's day-outing between Loughborough and Leicester in 1841 was the forerunner of the charter trips and package holidays of today.

One of the important effects of industrialisation as far as leisure activities are concerned is that there has been a change from participating to observing. Instead of taking part in sport or cultural activities people tend to watch others, often paid professionals. This is particularly true in the case of one of Britain's most popular entertainments, association football or 'soccer'.

In its original form football was (and indeed still is) widely played by amateur teams throughout the country. In 1888 the Football League was founded and it is from this that the multi-million pound game of today has grown. At the present time the Football League consists of ninety-two teams, graded into four divisions. While each team will have its devoted supporters who turn out to see their team in action each Saturday afternoon, the clubs that attract most attention are those in the First Division. Many First Division footballers are household names, sometimes enjoying the same kind of fame as film stars and pop singers. It is estimated that attendance at football matches is around the 19 million mark each season, while there are also large numbers of people who prefer to follow the sport on television. The climax of the year for both players and spectators is the Cup Final, played at the Wembley Stadium in London in early May. In addition to playing in league matches teams play other matches at home and abroad, while England, Wales, Scotland and Northern Ireland all have national teams that participate in international matches. In recent years attendances at matches have been falling off (perhaps due in part to the hooliganism that prevails at some games), but it is still true to say that football is the dominant Saturday afternoon entertainment between August and May, particularly in the north of England. Some, of course, prefer to play rather than watch, and there are something like a million amateur players in the country. The controlling body of Association Football in England is the Football Association, which was founded in 1863.

Rugby football is a game which seems to appeal mainly to English-speaking countries, although it is also played in France, Argentina and elsewhere. Rugby Union is confined to amateur clubs (there are about 1,600 in England), while Rugby League is played by professionals belonging to clubs concentrated in the north of England. Rugby Union is popular at many boys' schools (particularly public schools) and also at universities. International Rugby Union fixtures are often arranged, and there are county championships and other tournaments.

Like rugby football, cricket is largely confined to English-speaking countries (possibly, a cynic might say, because it is impossible to translate the rules). It is widely played in towns and villages throughout the country, while most schools, universities and many other institutions also have teams. There are nineteen 'first-class' teams: seventeen counties (playing in the County Championship) and the universities of Oxford and Cambridge. Each summer a 'Test' series is played between an England team and a touring side from overseas. When abroad the English team is known as the MCC, Marylebone Cricket Club, after the famous club, which drew up the laws of the game at the end of the eighteenth century. The governing body for cricket in

Britain is the Cricket Council, made up of a number of bodies representing the various groups interested in the game. In spite of its leisurely pace (a first-class county match can take three days and a Test match, five), the game has many devoted followers, both spectators and participants.

If cricket is England's national game, Scotland can lay claim to golf. Since the late nineteenth century, however, the 'Royal and Ancient Game' has spread south of the border and is now played in all parts of the United Kingdom. Some of the golf courses are owned by local authorities, but a large number are in the hands of private clubs, many of which charge high membership fees. Tennis courts are also owned by both municipalities and private clubs, the most famous of the latter being the All England Croquet and Lawn Tennis Club at Wimbledon. It is at Wimbledon that the open championships are played each year, and these usually attract leading players from all over the world.

Other sports that are popular in the United Kingdom include athletics, hockey, bowls and various kinds of water sport. Sailing has recently become very popular, both at coastal resorts and at inland centres, while rowing is practised on many rivers and inland lakes. Mountaineering and various types of hill-walking are also popular, particularly in Wales, the north of England and Scotland.

Hunting in Britain refers to the pursuit of wild animals by a pack of dogs and people either mounted or on foot, the most well-known branch of the sport being fox-hunting. In the west of England stag-hunting is still practised, while hares and otters are often used as quarry in other parts of the country. In recent years, hunting, along with other blood sports, has come in for considerable criticism, from those who feel that pursuing animals to their death is cruel and also from those who believe that many of the species hunted are in danger of extinction. Shooting – of game birds – is indulged in by landowners and others who can afford the high fees demanded by those who own shooting rights in various parts of the country. There is a certain amount of rough shooting in some areas, while wild-fowling is popular in coastal districts, particularly in East Anglia. There is also some deer-stalking in the Highlands of Scotland. The other popular 'field sport' is fishing and, as with shooting, most of the best areas are only available to those who purchase licences. Licences for 'coarse fishing' are inexpensive, and many stretches of river and canal banks are lined with rows of patient anglers during summer weekends and evenings.

Horse-racing is a sport with a large following. Basically there are two kinds of horse-racing in Britain: flat racing, from March to November, and steeplechasing, from August to June. While horse-racing attracts large crowds – the most fashionable meeting being that held at Ascot during June, 'Royal Ascot' – there is probably even more interest off the course in the 'betting shops' that can be found in every town in Britain. The betting shops exist to provide the punter with off-course gambling facilities, and they are licensed by the local authority. Many hunts hold point-to-point races to supplement their funds. Greyhound racing also has a large number of supporters, mainly in the big cities.

Every year a number of motor-car and motor-cycle meetings are held throughout the country. Perhaps the most important event for cars is the British Grand Prix, while each year the Tourist Trophy for motor cyclists is held in the Isle of Man. Rally driving has also attracted considerable interest in recent years, and the Royal Automobile Club arranges a nation-wide rally every year.

The government takes an active interest in promoting sport at various levels and there is a Minister for Sport, responsible for co-ordinating sporting activities. The national Sports Council advises the government on matters relating to amateur sport, while regional sports councils look after the interests of their areas. All schools are expected to provide facilities for physical recreation, and a large selection of sports are provided for. Most boys' schools will play either soccer or rugby football during the winter months and cricket during the summer, while some will also provide alternatives such as hockey. Girls will usually play hockey or netball during the winter and tennis or rounders in summer, although lacrosse is also found in some schools. At one time tennis seemed to be more popular at girls' schools than boys', but today most secondary schools provide some form of tennis facilities. Other sports found in schools include badminton, swimming – an increasing number of schools are acquiring their own swimming pools, often provided with the assistance of parents who are members of Parent-Teacher Associations – fencing and, of course, athletics.

The Theatre

There are some 300 professional theatres in the United Kingdom, over 40 of which are to be found in London and its suburbs. In the 'West End' (stretching roughly from Piccadilly to the Aldwych) some 30 theatres provide a wide range of plays, musicals and revues. The majority of

London's theatres are owned and run as business concerns, but the National Theatre, the Royal Shakespeare Company and the English Stage Company all receive sizeable subsidies. The National Theatre Company, founded after years of procrastination in 1963, now has a purpose-built theatre on the banks of the Thames. The Royal Shakespeare Company presents plays by Shakespeare at the Royal Shakespeare Theatre in Stratford-upon-Avon, the poet's birthplace, and a mixture of old and modern plays at the Barbican in the capital. Both the National Theatre and the RSC tour in Britain and overseas.

Until a few years ago theatre in the provinces was very much on the decline, as rising costs and shrinking audiences made the support of commercial theatres and theatre companies an extremely hazardous business. In the last decade or so, however, the situation has improved, and a number of new theatres have opened their doors, usually with Arts Council or local authority backing. Theatres, such as the Nottingham Playhouse, the Belgrade, Coventry, and the Phoenix, Leicester are striking modern buildings and present a wide range of plays. Many of the new theatres have attracted talented companies and leading directors, although on occasion there have been clashes between directors who are considered 'too advanced' and conservative theatre boards. Most of the civic theatres are repertory theatres, that is they rely on putting on a number of plays in a season, all with relatively short runs. There are also commercial theatres, some of which present plays prior to a London performance, and a few touring companies.

The problem facing many provincial theatres is to provide programmes that will appeal to a wide audience. Relatively few members of the population are interested in drama, while among those who are, there is much greater support for musicals, comedies and thrillers than modern or experimental drama. Nevertheless, most of the civic theatres do attempt to provide as wide a range as possible, and many run theatre weekends, training sessions and open houses in order to attract the public.

The Royal Opera House, Covent Garden, provides a home for the Royal Opera and the Royal Ballet. In addition to giving London seasons, both companies tour at home and abroad, although in practice the limited number of provincial theatres that can provide facilities for a major operatic production means that tours are often restricted in scope. The English National Opera Company also has its headquarters in London, and presents a season of opera each year during the winter.

During the summer the company makes a provincial tour. Other opera companies include the English Opera Group, the Welsh National Opera and the Scottish Opera. While the Royal Ballet is probably the best-known British ballet company, the Ballet Rambert is the oldest. Other ballet companies include London's Festival Ballet and the Scottish Theatre Ballet.

The United Kingdom has a number of well-known orchestras. London alone has five that enjoy a considerable international standing: the London Philharmonic, the London Symphony, the Royal Philharmonic, the New Philharmonia and the BBC Symphony. Outside the capital, the best-known orchestra is probably the Hallé, whose headquarters are in Manchester. In addition to the sympthony orchestras there are a number of chamber orchestras, such as the English Chamber Orchestra and the London Mozart Players. As in the case of the theatre, patronage of operas, ballet and concerts is confined to a small minority of the population, with the result that most companies and orchestras have to be supported by subsidies from the state and local authorities in order to survive.

Museums and art galleries are usually run by local authorities although national museums, such as the British Museum, the Science Museum and the National Gallery, are the responsibility of the Minister for the Arts. This Minister is in fact a parliamentary under-secretary known as the Minister for the Arts in the Department of Education and Science. In practice government funds are channelled through the Arts Council. Members of the Arts Council of Great Britain are appointed by the Secretary of State for Education and Science, and each year they are responsible for allocating funds to theatres, orchestras, opera and ballet companies and a variety of other cultural enterprises. Local authorities also contribute towards the arts, although many are criticised for not spending as much as they are entitled to out of the rates. Money from private sources and from industrial concerns also plays an important part in supporting artistic ventures, including festivals that take place all over the country. The most famous festival in the United Kingdom is probably the Edinburgh Festival, which is held each September. Other popular festivals include the City of London Festival, the Bath Festival and the Aldeburgh Festival.

In 1960 there were 3,034 cinemas in Great Britain; ten years later there were 1,529. In 1983 there were 1,500 screens in 803 cinemas, and admissions had dropped to 60 million. At the same time, the custom of watching films at home has become widely adopted in the last few years and it is estimated that 35 per cent of homes had home video-recorders in 1983.

Other Leisure Activities

In addition to the sporting and cultural activities outlined above, the British people engage in a wide range of other leisure-time activities. Traditionally the public house has been regarded as one of the main centres of British life outside working hours, and although a large number of pubs have suffered from attempts to give them a modern image, others strive to retain the atmosphere that made the pub an institution. Many pubs are 'tied houses', that is they are owned by breweries, and in some cases the owners have tried to establish a corporate image. Other innovations include juke boxes, fruit machines and canned music, often introduced at the expense of dart boards and other familiar features of the pub scene. Recently there have been some indications that the new image does not find universal acceptance and this has resulted in some modernisation programmes being modified.

Foreigners – and many British residents – have often criticised the licensing laws that govern pub opening hours and the sale of alcoholic drinks in the United Kindom. At present public houses are open for two or three hours at lunch time, and then from about 5.30 to 10.30 in the evening (precise times vary from area to area, and there are also special hours in force on market days or in special circumstances).

Although recommendations have been made that licensing laws should be made more flexible, apart from Scotland where bars are now permitted to be open most of the day, no new legislation has been passed to cover the rest of the United Kingdom.

In the past the pub often fulfilled the function of an informal club, and to a certain extent this remains true, particularly in rural areas. The pub was regarded as a male preserve, and women were only tolerated if they kept to the lounge or saloon bars. While many pubs concentrate on providing alcoholic beverages, others also provide food at the bar, or have restaurants attached.

Most workers in Britain are entitled to at least two weeks annual holiday with pay in addition to public holidays, and in many cases receive more than this. While many people take their holidays in Britain, the coasts, particularly those in the south and west, being very popular, an increasing number of holiday-makers are going abroad. It is estimated that between 7 and 8 million Britons travel overseas for holidays, the majority of them going to Spain, France and Italy. Charter flights and 'package tours' are usually well patronised, in spite of hair-raising stories about half finished hotels and inadequate food. Others prefer to travel independently using one of the many fast sea or air routes that link Britain with Europe.

In the past the British holiday was often spent at a guest house or small hotel at a seaside resort, or at that peculiarly British institution, the holiday camp. However, the increasing cost of accommodation and the lack of value for money in many places have driven more and more people to make their own arrangements, with the result that the caravaning or camping holiday has become extremely popular.

There is little doubt that the factor that has had most effect on the changing pattern of the British holiday is the increase in car ownership. Sixty per cent of households have the use of a car, while 15 per cent have two or more. The growth of car ownership, of course, has had a far-reaching effect on aspects of life other than holidays, for it has changed patterns of transport and involved the building of new roads and motorways.

Incomes

When the First World War broke out skilled male workers were earning an average wage of just under £100 a year. By 1924 average wages had risen to £180, but the economic difficulties of the late 1920s and early 1930s meant that skilled workers' average earnings only rose £15 between 1924 and 1935. After the Second World War earnings rose rapidly. The average for a skilled worker was £796 in 1960 and around £2,000 in 1974. Ten years later it was about £8,000. Other occupations have seen similar increases. In 1914 senior professionals, such as doctors, dentists and solicitors, were earning an average of £328 a year; by 1935 the average earnings in this group were £634 a year; while today senior managers, professionals and civil servants can earn between £20,000 and £30,000. Cabinet ministers draw a salary of £42,980 and senior company directors are in the same pay bracket.

Women have always tended to be paid less than men. In 1914 the skilled woman worker was paid an average of £44 a year and her sister in the professions an average of £89. Of course, at this time, the number of professional women was very small. Most were either teachers (average income for qualified women £104 per year) or nurses (average income £55 per year). By 1971 women manual workers were earning £820 per year, about half the amount that men were earning at that time. In spite of legislation to ensure similar pay for similar jobs women's pay still lags behind that of men – in mid-1984 the average gross weekly earnings for men was £173, or almost £9,000 a year, while the weekly figure for women was £115, or £6,000 a year.

The basic working week in the United Kingdom is between 35 to 40 hours, with non-manual workers tending to work shorter hours than manual workers. Office hours are usually between 9.00 a.m. and 5.00 p.m. or 5.30 p.m. with a lunch hour between 1.00 and 2.00 p.m. However, hours of work, length of holidays and rules about overtime differ from occupation to occupation and are the result of collective bargaining between employers and trade unions acting on behalf of employees, or individual negotiation.

In addition to the basic salary provided in monetary terms, some jobs carry extra benefits. These may be in the form of private pension schemes, sick pay arrangements, or participation in profit sharing or bonus schemes. Many managers will also receive benefits of other kinds, such as the provision of a company car, assistance with children's education, or loans made available at low rates of interest.

In October 1985 a study by Inbucon Management Consultants found that the average remuneration for managing directors in the United Kingdom was £41,029 a year. The average age of the managing directors was 49, they had been with their company for seventeen years and the salary range was from £23,500 in the smallest companies to £95,000 in the largest. The Inbucon study also found that the average UK executive was aged 45, had been in his present company for thirteen years, and earned £21,000. Nearly 80 per cent of managing directors and executives had company cars, while over 70 per cent had medical insurance.

Naturally, both basic earnings and any 'perks' are subject to taxation which is applied at a rate of 30 per cent on the first £15,400 of taxable income. There is a rate of 40 per cent on the £15,401–£18,200 band; 45 per cent on the £18,201–£23,100 band; 50 per cent on the £23,101–£30,600 band; 55 per cent on the £30,601–£38,000 band; and a rate of 60 per cent over £38,100. Tax relief is allowed for various purposes, the most important being for mortgage interest payments on loans made for house purchase. Income tax is by far the largest contributor to inland revenue funds, providing some 34·5 per cent of money raised by tax, compared with 18·4 per cent for VAT (currently imposed on most goods and services at a rate of 15 per cent), and 8·6 per cent for corporation tax.

The rapid increase in incomes since the Second World War has caused serious disquiet in government circles, for it has been felt that high wage costs coupled with poor productivity have had a detrimental effect on Britain's industrial performance. The Labour administration that was in power between 1945 and 1951 attempted to keep wages in check, but the policy became increasingly less effective following devaluation in 1949. During the 1950s a policy of persuasion was followed by the Conservatives, with varying success, while in 1962 pay increases were limited to a guideline of 2½ per cent. In 1963 the National Incomes Committee (NIC) was established, although it failed to receive co-operation from the trade unions. The Labour government elected in 1964 replaced the NIC by the National Board for Prices and Incomes and this body and accompanying legislation tended to slow down wage increases, but the trend for the decade was upwards. Restrictions on wage increases were removed by the incoming Heath government in 1970, with the result that prices and wages rocketed – a situation that was aggravated by the enormous increase in world oil prices that came into effect about the same time. When the Heath government was defeated over the miners' strike in 1974 the new Labour administration devised the social contract – a somewhat vague expression of intent that won the verbal support of the TUC and Labour politicians, but which had little real effect on salary increases. The Conservative Government which came to power in 1979 announced that wages and salaries should, like other parts of the economy, be governed by market forces. Thus government policy between 1979 and the present time has been to interfere only marginally in the process of establishing wage rates, apart from stating that these should not be higher than the rate of inflation. However, in certain cases, for example, the police, the armed forces, the judiciary and the civil service, large pay increases have been granted on the basis either of the inability of such groups to strike, or the national need. Other groups, notably the teachers, the railwaymen, miners and local government employees, have been resisted.

9

The Mass Media

Newspapers

England's first daily paper, the *Courant*, was published in 1702. During the course of the eighteenth century many more newspapers were founded, including the *Morning Post* in 1772 and *The Times* in 1785. However, it was not until the last decade of the nineteenth century that the mass circulation daily paper made its appearance.

In 1896 Alfred Harmsworth (later Lord Northcliffe) founded the *Daily Mail*, and by the beginning of the new century it was selling nearly a million copies a day. The *Mail* was to be the basis of a great newspaper empire that, at its height, included *The Times*, the *Observer*, the *Daily Mail*, the *Evening News*, the *Daily Mirror* (which, founded in 1903, in 1911 became the first daily paper to top the million mark in circulation) and a number of other weekly and provincial papers and periodicals. In 1900 Arthur Pearson started the *Morning Herald* (later renamed the *Daily Express*) which used techniques similar to those of the *Mail* with equal success.

The rise of the popular press at the end of the nineteenth and beginning of the twentieth centuries was the result of a number of factors. Whereas the newspapers of the mid-nineteenth century were directed primarily at the middle and upper classes, the *Daily Mail*, *Daily Express* and *Daily Mirror* were aimed, both in price and content, at the lower-middle and working classes. Using the most up-to-date printing methods, and obtaining a large revenue from advertising, Harmsworth was able to produce the *Daily Mail* more cheaply than its competitors. His distribution arrangements (from 1900 the paper was printed simultaneously in London and Manchester) ensured that he would get nationwide coverage. Another factor that should be taken into account is that the introduction of compulsory education in 1870 laid the foundations of universal literacy, which undoubtedly contributed to the success of the new papers. The growing political awareness of the working class and their desire to find out 'what was going on' should also be mentioned, although it was not until 1911 that the first socialist paper, the *Daily Herald*, appeared.

During the twentieth century, the number of newspaper readers has increased, although paradoxically the number of newspapers has declined. In 1921 there were 12 national morning papers, 21 national Sunday papers and 130 provincial papers (morning and evening). Some sixty years later there are 9 national morning papers, 8 national Sunday papers and some 120 provincial dailies or Sundays. In 1921 there were about 1,480 weekly papers; by the mid-1980s the figure was about 1,000. It is estimated that in 1920 just under 5.5 million newspapers were sold each day, compared with some 15 million national newspaper sales in the 1980s.

Britain is a relatively small country with good internal communications and it is largely due to this that a national press has developed. It is possible to buy a copy of one of the national papers virtually anywhere in the United Kingdom on the day it is published. National press in practice means London press, because although a number of national papers are printed in Manchester as well as London, all the national papers except one have their headquarters in the capital. The exception is *The Guardian*, founded as the *Manchester Guardian* in 1821, but even this paper now has editorial offices in London. Daily papers outside London are usually published as 'evening' papers and contain a mixture of national and local news. There are, however, a number of regional morning papers, such as the *Yorkshire Post*, the *Western Morning News* and the *Northern Echo*. Scotland has a number of newspapers in addition to those which come from England, the two leading ones being the *Scotsman* published in Edinburgh and the *Glasgow Herald* (Glasgow).

Although many of the leading newspapers have their editorial offices elsewhere, the congested London thoroughfare known as Fleet Street is justifiably regarded as the home of the British press, and over the years this name has become virtually synonymous with the national newspaper industry. One of the interesting characteristics of this industry is that, at any one time, over half the national newspapers seem in imminent danger of closure. Nor is this impression wholly without foundation, for in recent years a number of papers have ceased publication, both dailies – the *News Chronicle* and the *Daily Sketch*, and Sundays – the *Empire News*, the *Sunday Dispatch*, the *Sunday Citizen* and the *Sunday Graphic*. High circulations do not necessarily guarantee survival. More than 2 million copies of the *Empire News* were sold each Sunday, while the daily *News Chronicle* had a circulation of over 1 million.

Virtually every newspaper must supplement the income it receives from sales with revenue from other sources, and the most important of these is advertising. Advertising, however, cannot be entirely divorced from sales figures, as advertisers will only wish to buy space in papers that reach a large number of people. Thus a vicious circle sets in: newspapers with low circulations try to attract advertising to assist their finances and so develop means to improve their sales, but the advertisers are reluctant to use these papers. As circulation declines, so advertisers tend to fall away, which means that revenue continues to decrease. Unless another source of money is found, such as a subsidy, the proprietors will be forced to close down, merge with another paper – which usually amounts to the same thing – or sell to someone who is willing to invest money in a rescue operation. The financial structure of the newspaper industry in Britain is far from simple. In some cases a company will own a large range of papers and magazines, using the dull but solvent titles to support prestigious, but usually impecunious, big names, usually dailies or Sundays. It is by no means uncommon to find that many newspapers are controlled by large commercial groups with diversified interests, and once again the profitable sectors will help to carry the newspapers along. The involvement of large business enterprises in the production of newspapers and the concentration of ownership into a few hands has caused considerable concern in recent years.

There have been no less than three Royal Commissions on the Press since the end of the Second World War – in 1949, 1962 and 1974 – looking into issues such as the concentration of ownership of the national press into the hands of large corporations and similar problems. None of the findings of the Royal Commissions have had much effect on the structure of the newspaper industry, however, and the buying and selling of newspapers has continued unabated, particularly in the 1980s. Following a lengthy stoppage, due to an industrial dispute over manning, the Thomson Group, owners of Times Newspapers, sold *The Times* and the *Sunday Times* to News International, which already owned a national daily – *The Sun* – and a Sunday – the *News of the World*. Pergamon Press bought the Mirror Group – the *Daily Mirror*, the *Sunday Mirror* and the *Sunday People* – in 1984, while the following year control of the *Sunday Telegraph* and the *Daily Telegraph* passed into the hands of a Canadian financier, Conrad Black, while Express Newspapers, publishers of two dailies – the *Daily Express* and the *Daily Star* – and a Sunday – the *Sunday Express* – came under the ownership of United Newspapers. New ownership has, in certain cases, seen the introduction of new methods of production and a subsequent confrontation between management and print unions. Such disputes have caused great interest not only among the unions and management of other existing companies who are, of course, anxious to know how the outcome will affect them, but also a number of other would-be 'press barons' who are making plans for new national papers.

The British national press can be divided roughly into two sections, the 'qualities' or 'heavies', and the 'populars', although such a division is far from absolute. Among the dailies, *The Times*, the *Daily Telegraph*, *The Guardian* (plus the specialised *Financial Times*, which concentrates on 'City' news) are considered to be 'qualities'. The *Daily Mirror*, the *Daily Express*, the *Daily Mail* and *The Sun* can be classified as 'popular' papers. The division is made primarily on the basis of how each paper treats the news. The 'qualities' usually have in-depth news items, backed up by articles written by staff writers or outsiders interpreting the news. The 'populars' give space to relatively few news stories, and those that they do cover are often treated superficially. The popular papers also tend to have more photographs than the qualities, and in many cases these are included for their decorative value, rather than their relevance to the news.

In March 1986 a new daily called *Today* made its appearance. The paper utilised new methods of production and distribution and included colour photographs as a regular feature. It was followed by *The Independent* in October 1986.

When one looks at the circulation figures (see Table 9.1) it is immediately apparent that the sales performance of the populars is decidedly better than that of the qualities. However, the qualities not only cost more, they also carry far more of the revenue-earning classified advertising. Over 30 per cent of the *Daily Telegraph*, for example, is made up of pages carrying 'classifieds' (small advertisements closely set in columns under classifications such as 'For Sale', 'Wanted', and so on), compared with about 4 per cent for the *Daily Express* and less than 1 per cent for the *Daily Mirror*. A comparable situation exists with the Sundays. The qualities – the *Sunday Times*, *The Observer* and the *Sunday Telegraph* – all carry more advertising than editorial matter, a great deal of it in the form of

Table 9.1 *Circulation of National Newspapers*

	Oct.85– March 86	Oct. 84– March 85	% change (–)
Sun	4,125,475	4,060,441	1.6
Mirror	3,014,464	3,389,728	(11.1)
Daily Star	1,399,036	1,555,406	(10.1)
Daily Express	1,886,408	1,943,271	(2.9)
Daily Mail	1,800,200	1,844,617	(2.4)
Daily Telegraph	1,175,811	1,226,359	(4.1)
Guardian	507,806	485,391	4.6
Times	471,162	467,763	0.7
Financial Times	240,493	224,931	6.9
News of the World	4,979,074	4,750,346	4.8
Sunday Mirror	3,030,207	3,331,526	(9.0)
Sunday People	3,027,382	3,147,224	(3.8)
Sunday Express	2,415,895	2,479,190	(2.6)
Mail on Sunday	1,613,440	1,615,828	(0.2)
Sunday Times	1,226,909	1,271,393	(3.5)
Observer	762,672	754,986	1.0
Sunday Telegraph	677,536	695,056	(2.5)

Source: ABC
Figures for *Today* and *The Independent* were not available as both were founded in 1986.

classified advertisements. As in the quality dailies, the emphasis is on giving the background to the news, and all three papers contain articles of considerable length, analysing different aspects of home or foreign events. The popular Sundays – the *News of the World*, the *Sunday People*, the *Sunday Mirror* and the *Sunday Express* – are more concerned with 'human interest' stories and photographs. Like the qualities they carry advertising, but the emphasis is on display advertisements rather than classifieds.

In addition to carrying news and advertisements, the newspapers also have feature articles, reviews, sports pages and financial and business sections, although the proportions devoted to each of these vary considerably from one paper to another. Although some of the Sundays have names resembling those of daily papers, and are indeed owned by the same group, the papers retain their own identities. Thus the *Sunday Express* and the *Daily Express* are both owned by United Newspapers, but each has its own editor and staff. The same is true of *The Times* and the *Sunday Times*, both part of the News International Group, and the *Daily Mirror* and *Sunday Mirror* published by the International Publishing Corporation. *Today* is published seven days a week. Apart from the *Morning Star* which is controlled by the Communist Party, none of the national papers is owned by a political party although this does not mean, of course, that they do not have political opinions. Politically speaking, the majority of the British press is inclined to be right of centre. The left-wing *Daily Herald* mentioned earlier changed its name, ownership and outlook during the 1960s, rising again as the *Sun*.

Something like 4,200 periodicals are published in the United Kingdom, covering a very wide range of topics. The leading serious weeklies are the *New Statesman, The Economist* and the *Spectator*, which provide coverage of national and international affairs from different points of the political spectrum. They also have sections dealing with the arts. *Punch* is well known as an old-established humorous weekly, while the irreverent *Private Eye*, founded during the 1960s, maintains a somewhat precarious existence sniping at the more pompous features of British life. Women's periodicals, such as *Woman* and *Woman's Own*, enjoy a wide circulation, as do many of the magazines catering for leisure activities. Although there are a large number of well-illustrated magazines dealing with subjects as varied as gardening, railways, cooking, architecture and attractive girls, Britain has no illustrated news magazines of the *Paris-Match* or *Stern* type. *Picture Post*, which enjoyed great popularity during the 1940s, was unable to survive the competition of television, while attempts to launch new magazines of this type have proved unsuccessful.

Radio and Television

The first commercial broadcasting to be carried out in Britain was when the Marconi Company was given permission to transmit for one hour a day from radio station 2 LO. In December 1922 Mr John Reith (later Lord Reith) was appointed General Manager of the British Broadcasting Company, and in 1927 he became Director-General of the new British Broadcasting Corporation. Reith was to have great effect on how the BBC carried out its duties. In his opinion it was the BBC's responsibility to give the public, not what they wanted, but what 'they ought to want'. As the BBC was in a monopoly position this in practice meant that the public had to accept what the Corporation and its director-general thought was good for them. Reith was also very concerned that the BBC should retain its independence of the government and commercial interests. Before long the BBC built up a considerable reputation for impartiality in its news reports, and this was enhanced during the Second World War by the radio reports beamed to occupied Europe.

Until the 1950s the BBC had a monopoly of broadcasting in Britain, but with the advent of television there was considerable pressure from commercial interests to establish other firms with permits to broadcast. Largely owing to the tactics of a small but extremely well-organised pressure group, the commercial lobby won the day, and in March 1954 the Bill to establish an 'independent' television authority was passed. Fourteen months later the first programmes containing advertising spots were broadcast.

At the present time the BBC controls two national television services, four national radio services and a number of local radio stations. The Independent Broadcasting Authority (originally the Independent Television Authority) controls the activities of the commercial television companies and radio companies. The BBC has a board of governors who, under their chairman, are responsible for supervising the programmes that are transmitted. These governors are appointed by the Crown, on the advice of the government. The day-to-day running of the BBC is in the hands of the director-general, who is chosen by the board of governors. The BBC is financed by a grant from Parliament, which is derived from the revenue received from the sale of television licences. The BBC also gets revenue from selling programmes to overseas television companies, and from the sale of books, magazines and other publications, including the *Radio Times*. The BBC's external services also receive government support.

The Independent Broadcasting Authority consists of a chairman and ten other members appointed by the Minister of Posts and Telecommunications. The IBA does not produce programmes itself, but issues licences to, and supervises, the transmitting companies. It also owns Channel 4.

There are fifteen programme companies making up Independent Television (ITV), for example Thames (London), Granada (North West) and Anglia (East Anglia), that hold contracts to provide programmes for the fourteen regions into which Britain is divided. (London has two companies, of which one provides programmes during the week, the other at weekends.) The IBA is financed by rental received from programme companies for use of transmitting facilities. Every six years the contracts granted to programme companies are reviewed; each company has to apply for a renewal of its licence, while new companies are invited to apply at the same time. The programme companies receive nothing from licence fees, and are entirely dependent on the money they get from advertising. In 1972 the Sound Broadcasting Act was passed, ending the BBC's monopoly of radio broadcasting. It is envisaged that there will eventually be a network of up to sixty local stations operating on a commercial basis. Some of the strongest criticism of commercial radio on a local basis has come from local and regional newspapers, and it is interesting to note that an effort has been made to give newspapers a share in the ownership of the stations. At the same time measures have been taken to ensure that control of the media is not concentrated into too few hands. The local newspapers' objection to local commercial radio was largely due to the fear that the radio stations would take away the advertising that provides the newspapers with a great deal of their revenue.

Television viewing is the most popular leisure activity in Britain. Virtually all households have a television set, while 35 per cent have two or more receivers. A large proportion of the programmes shown are produced in Britain, although there are a number of American series on both BBC and ITV. A few programmes come from other countries, Australia, for example, but very few foreign-language productions reach the screen as the British seem to object to subtitles.

The range of programmes shown varies considerably in quality. There are a number of current affairs, educational, sport, and cultural programmes and a wide selection of plays, series, films and variety shows. Owing to the competition that exists between the BBC and ITV there is often a tendency for similar programmes to be broadcast at the same time, for example, one channel may be producing a variety show, which leads to the other channel having a variety show at the same time, with what it considers to be bigger and better stars.

In 1964 the BBC was granted a second television channel, BBC 2, giving it what ITV regarded as an unfair advantage. It was the intention of the BBC that programmes on BBC 2 would include a high proportion of minority interest programmes, and although this happens in some cases (for example, the Open University programmes are transmitted on BBC2) there is evidence that at peak viewing times the battle of the ratings ónce again becomes of key importance (the ratings show how many people watch each programme).

Channel 4 – the second ITV channel – commenced transmission in November 1982. It provides a television service throughout the country (with the exception of Wales where the service is in the hands of Sianel 4 Cymru which ensures that a high proportion of the output of the service is in Welsh), and is financed by subscriptions from the independent television companies in return for advertising time. Like BBC 2, Channel 4 provides a considerable number of documentary and educational programmes and has also been responsible for the production of some striking films and plays. In February 1983, TV-AM – broadcasting throughout the country for three hours at breakfast time – after a somewhat shaky start established itself as a strong competitor to the BBC 1 breakfast programme which had started a month earlier.

Opinions about the standard of programmes shown on British television differ widely. It is probably true to say that some of the news and current affairs reporting is of a very high standard, while there are also excellent drama productions which enable many people to see plays they would not be able to see in the theatre. On a number of occasions there have been attempts by self-appointed protectors of public morals to influence the kind of programmes broadcast on television, but there seems little evidence that the British public is exposing itself to great moral danger by sitting in front of the television screen for some twenty hours a week (the average viewing time per head of population).

10

Religious Life

Christianity came to Britain in Roman times although its influence declined after the withdrawal of the legions early in the fifth century. In 596 Pope Gregory sent a party of monks led by Augustine to convert the English and it was these men and their successors who established the position of the Roman Catholic Church in this country. Throughout the Middle Ages, the English kings acknowledged at least nominal allegiance to Rome, but by the sixteenth century it was clear that relations were becoming somewhat strained. In 1534 Henry VIII broke with Rome, the immediate cause of the breach being the Pope's refusal to recognise his divorce from Catherine of Aragon. Although his elder daughter, Mary Tudor, tried to re-establish the Roman Catholic Church in England during her reign (1553–8), she was unsuccessful. Her sister Elizabeth had been brought up a Protestant and the Settlement made soon after she came to the throne confirmed the position of the Protestant Church of England. The Elizabethan Church Settlement, however, did not end religious controversy in Britain, as even the most cursory glance at the history books will show. Matters of faith were rarely far from the minds of those involved in the conflicts of the seventeenth century, although once again the Church of England triumphed when the Protestant William III replaced the Catholic James II on the throne in 1688. Throughout the eighteenth century Nonconformists and Roman Catholics were barred from holding public office, but the 1828 Test Act and the 1829 Catholic Emancipation Act lifted many of the restrictions laid upon those who were not members of the Anglican Church.

The Church of England

The Church of England is still the established Church in England. (In Wales the Church of England was disestablished in 1920, largely because the Welsh have a strong Nonconformist tradition.) The head of the Church of England is the monarch and part of the coronation ceremony includes an oath in which the monarch promises to protect the position of the Anglican Church. Archbishops, bishops and deans are appointed by the Crown, although in fact the advice of the Prime Minister is the decisive factor. The involvement of the Prime Minister is interesting because although the monarch must be a member of the Church of England by law, the Prime Minister need not be a member of the Anglican or indeed any other Church. (It seems likely that this method of appointing senior members of the Church will be changed in the near future.)

The links between Church and state can also be seen in the fact that archbishops and twenty-four other bishops sit in the House of Lords and participate in debates on equal terms with members of the peerage. Unlike other members of the upper house, however, they do not sit for life, giving up their seats when they retire from their sees. The Church of England must obtain parliamentary approval if it wishes to change its form of worship, and this approval is by no means always forthcoming. In 1929 the Church Assembly produced a revised prayer book, which was accepted by the House of Lords, but rejected by the Commons. As the Church as a whole was in favour of the new prayer book, the action of the Commons raised the whole question of the position of the state Church, and there were those who suggested that disestablishment was the answer. The question of disestablishment has also come up more recently. In 1970 a commission set up to consider the relationship between Church and state recommended that the status of the Church of England should be maintained, but that a number of changes should be introduced to give the Church more autonomy. The most important of these proposals were that the Church should have final authority over its forms of doctrine and worship, so avoiding a repetition of the 1929 situation; that the methods of selecting bishops should be revised; that all ministers of religion should be able to stand for Parliament; and that leading members of other churches should be invited to sit in the House of Lords, alongside the senior bishops of the Church of England. Some people felt that the commission did not go far enough, and should have recommended a complete break between Church and state, while others felt that the changes proposed were too radical to be acceptable.

England is divided into two provinces, Canterbury and York, and forty-three dioceses, twenty-nine of which are in the Province of Canterbury, while the remaining fourteen come under the authority of the Archbishop of York. Although the Archbishop of Canterbury and the Archbishop of York are nominally of equal status, in practice the former, who is styled 'Primate of All England', is the senior, and is in fact the professional head of the Anglican Church. Many of the bishoprics are of considerable antiquity; Canterbury was first established at the end of the sixth century by St Augustine, while others, such as Leicester and Guildford, set up in 1926 and 1927 respectively, were founded to meet the needs of present centres of population. In the older dioceses the bishop has his seat in an ancient cathedral. Most of these cathedrals were built during the Middle Ages and they embody a fascinating variety of styles, sometimes providing an outline of several centuries of English architecture in one building. The majority of the medieval cathedrals are extremely impressive buildings, even more so when one takes into account the relatively primitive technology of those responsible for designing and erecting them. In the case of dioceses of more recent foundation the cathedral is usually a large parish church adapted to suit the responsibilities of its new status, examples being Leicester, Manchester and Derby. In some dioceses, however, notably Truro, Liverpool, Guildford and Coventry, new cathedrals have been built in the last hundred years or so.

There are about 13,500 ecclesiastical parishes in England, each centred on a parish church. Most parishes have a resident parish priest, while a large town parish will probably also have one or more assistant priests or curates. In early Christian times the founder of a parish had the privilege of appointing the parish priest, this right of patronage being known as the advowson. During the Middle Ages many advowsons were in the possession of monasteries, and when these were dissolved by Henry VIII the advowsons passed into the hands of the Crown, or lay landowners who had bought monastic land. Today patronage is exercised by bishops and archbishops, cathedral chapters, the Crown, lay landowners – including some large companies – the universities, particularly Oxford and Cambridge colleges, and trusts. In February 1975 the General Synod of the Church voted to end the old system of patronage and to give the Church more control. Most livings are supported by endowments and sometimes by land known as a glebe. Other sources of income are fees for services, such as marriages and funerals, while the parish priest is also entitled to the proceeds of the Easter Collection. Incumbents of livings where the endowment is insufficient may receive assistance from central funds of the Church or a stewardship scheme arranged by parishioners.

The Church of England does not have a formal register of members. One becomes a member of the Church on baptism, and this membership is often re-endorsed at confirmation, usually at the age of 14 or so. An electoral roll, consisting of parishioners over the age of 16, is compiled every year, usually at the Easter communion. However, having one's name on the electoral role is not necessarily proof of active Church membership, nor does it impose any compulsory duties, such as payment of a church tax. In these circumstances it is not surprising that any accurate measurement of membership of the Church of England is virtually impossible. It has been estimated that over 27 million of the population of England have been baptised into the Church, almost 10 million have been confirmed, while 2·5 million appear on the electoral rolls. The appearance of a name on the roll does not necessarily mean that the elector plays an active part in parish activities by taking advantage of the right to vote for parish officials, or standing for election. Church attendance is also difficult to estimate, although few would dispute that Church of England congregations, like those of the other Churches, have declined during the present century. Some 1·7 million people attended Christmas and Easter communion services in 1982.

Although the Church of England is the state Church it receives no financial assistance from the government, apart from salaries paid to chaplains in the armed forces and money provided for Church schools. The main financial support for the Church comes from the free-will offerings of Church members and from its own land and capital. Although the amount of land held by the Church has shrunk from its heyday just before the Reformation, the Church of England is still the third largest landowner in the country, after the Forestry Commission and the Crown. The assets of the Church are administered by the Church Commissioners, who by wise investment on the Stock Exchange have managed to increase the income of the Church by a considerable amount in recent years. Nevertheless, there are many demands on the resources of the Church, including salaries, the upkeep of ancient churches and cathedrals and the financing of various services provided by the Church at home and overseas.

Between 1919 and 1970 the governing body of the Church of England was the Church Assembly, but in September 1970 elections were held for the new General Synod of the Church. The General Synod, which is composed of the bishops, and representatives of the clergy and laity deals with matters such as education, missions, social questions, training for the ministry, interchurch relations and the care of church buildings.

The clergy of the Church of England are all male, but in 1984 the General Synod voted in favour of legislation being prepared to enable women to be ordained as priests. However, there is considerable opposition to this idea among both lay and ordained members of the Church and it seems that it will be many years before women are permitted to perform all the priestly functions.

In addition to the Church of England in England, the Anglican Communion extends to other parts of the British Isles and throughout the world. The (unestablished) Church of Wales is headed by the Archbishop of Wales, and there are also the Episcopal Church in Scotland and the rather misleadingly named Church of Ireland, which covers both Northern Ireland and the Irish Republic. Every tenth year the Lambeth Conference (Lambeth Palace is the London residence of the Archbishop of Canterbury) meets, and is attended by Anglican bishops from all over the world. The conference has no executive authority, but provides a useful forum for the exchange of ideas.

The Church of Scotland

The Church of Scotland took its Presbyterian form after the Reformation, and maintained its opposition to episcopacy (rule by bishops) throughout the seventeenth century, in spite of Charles I's attempts to remodel it on the lines of the Church of England. The status of the Church of Scotland was confirmed by the Treaty of Union between England and Scotland in 1707. The Church of Scotland, which has the sovereign in her capacity as Queen of Scotland at its head, is completely free from parliamentary control. All ministers of the Church are of equal status, although each year a Moderator is elected to preside over the meeting of the General Assembly, which consists of elected ministers and elders of the Kirk. Each of the 1,700 or so churches is under the local control of the Kirk Session (the ministers and elders of the church), while above this is the Court of the Presbytery, the Court of Synod and the General Assembly. Adult membership of the Church of Scotland is about 900,000.

The Roman Catholic Church

After the Reformation the Roman Catholic Church in England suffered considerable hardships. By the nineteenth century, however, attitudes had mellowed somewhat and the hierarchy was reintroduced to England in 1850 and to Scotland in 1878. At the present time there are 7 Roman Catholic provinces, 29 episcopal dioceses and some 3,000 parishes. The head of the Roman Catholic Church in England is the Archbishop of Westminster. It is estimated that the Roman Catholic Church has nearly 6 million members in Britain, the majority of whom live in large towns.

Recently there have been many discussions between the Roman Catholic Church and members of other churches in Britain, as elsewhere in the world, on the subject of co-operation; and a number of interdenominational services have been held. The age-old distrust between Protestants and Catholics seems to have died down in most parts of Britain, although the past, or a highly coloured version of the past, is still remembered in Scotland, while the tragedy of Northern Ireland shows that for some the past and present are inextricably linked.

The Free Churches

The Methodist Church, which today has some 500,000 members, was founded by a Church of England clergyman called John Wesley. At first Wesley tried to maintain his links with the Anglican Church, but the opposition of the hierarchy of that institution to his methods and his doctrine forced him to break away in 1784 and ordain his own clergy. A number of divisions occurred within the Methodist Church during the nineteenth century, but most of the schisms were healed in 1932. In the 1960s and again in 1972 an attempt was made to bring together the Methodist and Anglican Churches. Although the proposal was accepted by the Methodists, it failed to get the necessary majority from the Anglicans, and so the idea came to nothing. Individual Methodist churches have a considerable degree of self-government, and each year a conference, which is chaired by an elected president is held to discuss matters of concern to the church.

In 1972 the oldest community of Dissenters in Britain, the Congregationalists, united with the English Presbyterian Church to form the United Reformed Church. Other Christian groups represented in Britain include the Baptists, who have about 2,000 churches, the Society of Friends (Quakers), first active in the mid-seventeenth century, the Salvation Army, founded by William Booth in 1865, and the Unitarian Church.

The Jewish community in Britain is divided into two groups, the Orthodox, consisting of about 80 per cent of practising Jews, and the Reform, which originated during the last century. The leading member of the Jewish community is the Chief Rabbi, who belongs to the Orthodox group. The Jewish community numbers about 410,000, and it has 240 synagogues, mainly in urban areas.

Since the Second World War large-scale immigration into the United Kingdom has meant that there are substantial Muslim (estimated to be 1·2 million), Hindu and Sikh communities throughout the country.

11

England and Ireland

The national flag of Britain consists of the three flags associated with the saints of England, Scotland and Ireland superimposed upon each other to form the Union Flag (sometimes incorrectly termed the Union Jack), thus symbolising the unity of the three countries. However, as is often the case with symbolism, this flag raises as many questions as it answers, in particular, why should Ireland, independent since 1922, still form an essential part of it? Clearly, it is not possible in this book to look at the whole history of the relationship between the Irish and the other nationalities inhabiting the British Isles, but it is probably appropriate to look at some of the main features of Anglo-Irish history in order to focus on the troubles that have been a feature of life in Northern Ireland since 1969.

The first large-scale invasion of Ireland by the English took place in 1166 when a force of Norman knights under the leadership of Strong-bow, the Earl of Pembroke, went to the aid of Dermot MacMurrough, King of Leinster. The invasion was backed by King Henry II who took the title Lord of Ireland – a role that he and his successors honoured more in the breach than in the observance. Throughout the Middle Ages the affairs of Ireland were of relatively little importance to their nominal English rulers and the Irish developed their own customs and culture. Thus, at the time of the Reformation, when the Protestant religion was adopted in England, Wales and Scotland, the Irish insisted on remaining Catholics, and during the seventeenth century this tenacious hold of the Irish on their faith led them into armed clashes with their English overlords. After the Civil War in England, the Lord Protector, Oliver Cromwell, led a force to crush the remaining supporters of Charles I and during the ensuing campaign he massacred the inhabitants of the towns of Wexford and Drogheda. Cromwell was, of course, a staunch Protestant and his victims were Catholics. In 1690, William of Orange, invited to become the Protestant King of

England in place of the deposed Catholic monarch, James II, defeated James's Franco-Irish army at the Battle of the Boyne, thus securing the Protestant Succession and a heroic place in the history of Protestant Ireland. Whereas the vast majority of the Irish population were Catholics, there were a number of Protestants who were concentrated almost exclusively in an area roughly co-terminal with the ancient kingdom of Ulster. Most of these Protestants had been encouraged to move from England and the lowlands of Scotland by Elizabeth I and Cromwell, through grants of land and favoured treatment over the native Irish.

Once the Protestant Succession had been secured, measures were taken throughout the British Isles to ensure that Catholics were excluded from positions of power and authority. The impact on Ireland was particularly marked: Catholics were forbidden to hold official positions, were not allowed to serve in the armed forces, and had restrictions placed upon them as far as land purchase and tenure were concerned. This meant that Irish land was owned mainly by Englishmen or Scots, who were either Protestants from Ulster or, more often than not, absentee landlords. Although Ireland retained her Parliament, Catholics were not allowed to sit in it and the English Parliament had a right of veto over all measures passed by the Irish one. The English Parliament also imposed restrictive trading laws on the Irish which meant that the Irish economy was unable to develop. These conditions prevailed throughout most of the eighteenth century, although certain restrictions were lifted in the last two decades. It was not until 1829, however, that the Catholic Emancipation Act – giving Catholics the right to hold public office – was passed and then only after bitter opposition from sectors of the English parliament. If the struggle for Catholic Emancipation dominated the politics of the first three decades of the nineteenth century, the Home Rule question dominated the final two. Although the passing of the Catholic Emancipation Act allowed Irish Catholics to become involved in the government of their country by sending MPs to Westminster (the separate Irish Parliament had been abolished in 1801) conditions had not improved. During the 1840s the Irish potato famine had a catastrophic effect on the population of the country reducing it, through a combination of death through starvation and emigration, from 8 million in 1841 to 6 million at the end of the decade. The continuing discontent in Ireland manifested itself in rebellions, bombings – both in Ireland and on the mainland – and through parliamentary agitation by the Nationalist MPs sitting in

Westminster. By and large, English government ministers and the bulk of the English people tended to regard the Irish with a mixture of scorn and exasperation and any action taken to deal with the Irish problem tended to be too little or too late.

However, by the 1880s, it became clear that some action would have to be taken and in 1886 the Liberal Prime Minister, W. E. Gladstone, introduced a Home Rule Bill, which, if passed, would have restored a measure of self-government to Ireland. The Bill, however, was bitterly opposed by the Tory Party – who declared themselves to be 'Unionists' and the Bill was defeated to the chagrin of the Irish Nationalists and to the delight of the Conservatives and the Protestants of Ulster, who saw in Irish Home Rule a threat to their economic and political power. A second Home Rule Bill, introduced in 1893, suffered the same fate as its predecessor at the hands of the Conservative-dominated House of Lords, as did the third Bill which was introduced in 1912. However, by this date the rules of the game had been altered through the Parliament Act of 1911 under which the Lords no longer had the power to defeat Bills already passed by the Commons. The Irish Nationalists therefore looked forward to the passing of the Home Rule Bill in 1914, while the Ulstermen in the North began to arm themselves to resist what they considered to be an imminent invasion from the South. Groups of Nationalists, who over the years had shown that they were no strangers to the politics of armed struggle, formed their own armed units and by the beginning of 1914 it looked as if Ireland were on the brink of civil war. However the danger of such a conflict was averted by the outbreak of a greater one – the First World War. The Irish Nationalists sitting at Westminster – presumably thinking, like other groups, that the war would be of short duration – agreed that the Home Rule Bill should be held in abeyance until the war was over. Other groups within Ireland, however, were less inclined to be patient and in Easter 1916 the Easter Rebellion broke out in Dublin. By all accounts, the rebellion lacked popular support but the English authorities, concerned about the effect which such an event might have in the middle of a war, over-reacted and the leaders of the rebellion were brought to trial and executed. There was an immediate outcry and the cause of Irish independence gained momentum.

Attempts to reach a compromise agreement failed and guerilla warfare broke out between the forces of the Nationalists and the Royal Irish Constabulary. In the 1918 general election the Home Rulers were virtually ousted by Sinn Fein (Ourselves Alone) who won seventy-three of the 105 seats in Ireland. The newly elected Sinn Fein members refused to take their seats at Westminster and set up their own parliament – the Dail Eireann – in Dublin, while the fighting between the nationalists and the British forces intensified. By now the police had been reinforced by Auxiliaries and the 'Black and Tans' (recruited from the British armed forces). They and the nationalist forces (known as the Irish Republican Army – the IRA) waged a bitter struggle of terror and counter-terror. In 1920 in an attempt to end the fighting Westminster passed the Government of Ireland Act which made provision for two parliaments in Ireland, one in the north, the other in the south, with a Council of Ireland to encourage cooperation, consultation and eventually union between them. However, at elections held in May 1921 Sinn Fein again won virtually all the seats in the south and assembled once again in Dublin. In July 1921 a truce to the fighting was agreed and the following October a conference was convened in London. Two months later it was announced that the Irish Free State was to be established, with the status of a dominion within the British Empire. Northern Ireland was given a month to decide whether it wanted to join the Free State or remain part of the United Kingdom. The treaty was accepted by the Dail in January 1922 but many of the nationalists rejected the idea of dominion status and refused to accept it. Civil war broke out between the 'treaty forces' and the 'Irregulars', southern Irish against southern Irish with the British and the Northern Irish standing on the side-lines. After a brief but bitter struggle the rebels were defeated and the Irish Free State came into existence, with the six counties of Ulster choosing to remain part of the United Kingdom.

Between 1922 and 1938 the remaining ties between Britain and southern Ireland were loosened. The Free State remained neutral in the Second World War, and in 1949 the Republic formally left the Commonwealth.

During the 1950s and 1960s relations between Britain and the Republic gradually improved and in 1965 the Irish Prime Minister, Sean Lemass, made an official visit to Ulster – a visit that was returned shortly afterwards by Terence O'Neill, the Prime Minister of Northern Ireland. However, the majority of the population of the North, some 67 per cent of whom were Protestant, remained implacably opposed to closer ties with the Republic. Moreover, many Catholics in Ulster felt that they were discriminated against in the fields of housing and job opportunities and during the late 1960s the Civil Rights movement grew increasingly strident in its demands for more equitable treatment. Inevitably there were clashes between the activists and the police, who were seen, with some justification, as being the personification of Protestant power. There was particular antipathy between the demonstrators and the police reservists, known as the 'B' Specials and, as violence grew, pressure was put on the Westminster government to intervene. In August 1969 the British army was ordered into Ulster to take over the security role from the Ulster Constabulary. For a brief period the army was welcomed by the Catholic population, but the honeymoon was very brief and, rather than improving, the situation swiftly deteriorated. During the Irish civil war of the early 1920s, the opposition to those who had signed the Treaty with Britain was led, as we have seen, by a group calling itself the Irish Republican Army. Although defeated by the Irish government, the IRA had never completely disappeared and indeed during the 1940s and 1950s had been involved in terrorist activities in both mainland Britain and the Irish Free State. Now, the troubles in Ulster gave the IRA a chance to strike at its old enemy once again. However, the older generation of IRA men were disinclined to undertake active operations against the British army and have, on the whole, remained aloof from the fighting that has taken place over the last fifteen years. Most of the responsibility for attacks on the security forces and other targets has fallen to the 'Provisional IRA' – as opposed to the older-established 'Official' IRA, and a variety of other nationalist groups.

Terence O'Neill, who had been Prime Minister of Ulster throughout the 1960s resigned in 1969 and was replaced by James Chichester-Clark. Both of these men, as well as the overwhelming majority of MPs in the Ulster Parliament at Stormont (as well as the Ulster representatives at Westminster), represented the Unionist cause – based firmly on the concept of Protestant supremacy. Opposition to the Unionists was in the hands of the Social Democrat and Labour Party (SDLP), and the Alliance Party which was formed in 1971 in an attempt to form a bridge between Catholics and Protestants. (It should be noted that, in spite of having similar names to parties on the mainland, the Northern Ireland parties have no formal link with either the Social Democratic Party or the Alliance Party represented at Westminster.)

In 1971 Chichester-Clark resigned and was succeeded by Brian Faulkner who was destined to be the last Prime Minister of the Ulster Parliament. During the second half of 1971 and early 1972 the scale of violence grew and in one incident twelve demonstrators were killed by

British soldiers firing into a crowd from which they claimed shots had come. 'Bloody Sunday', as this incident was named, exacerbated an already deteriorating situation. In March 1972 the Ulster Parliament was suspended and the Stormont government resigned. Edward Heath, who was then the British Prime Minister, appointed a British Cabinet minister, William Whitelaw, as the first Secretary of State for Northern Ireland with direct responsibility for Ulster. During 1973 attempts were made to bring together the opposing factions in Ulster to work out a basis for the future government and organisation of Northern Ireland, Politicians from the various Unionist groups, the SDLP and the Alliance Party were all invited to talks, but little progress was made. The basic problem at the heart of the Ulster situation is that the Protestant majority are completely opposed to any solution that will bring them under the rule of Dublin. They also refuse to take part in any negotiations that will bring them into contact with any of the Nationalist organisations pledged to a united Ireland. The Unionists, as their name implies, see their security resting on the maintenance of the link with mainland Britain, although some Protestants have gone on record as saying that they would prefer independence and a complete break with the United Kingdom to being incorporated into the Irish Republic. For their part, British governments, of both right and left, have said that they will not agree to any settlement that will bring about a united Ireland against the wishes of the majority of the population in Ulster. Against such a background it is not surprising that a decade of discussion and attempts at new initiatives have led nowhere.

In 1974 a power-sharing executive, headed by the former Prime Minister of Northern Ireland, Brian Faulkner, was established but it was brought down by the Ulster (Protestant) Workers' strike in May and Direct Rule was resumed. The following year elections were held for a seventy-eight seat convention, but this initiative also failed and discussions were wound up in March 1976.

The following month the 1,500th death since violence broke out in 1969 was recorded. There were signs during 1977 and 1978 that the situation was improving slightly – a strike called by the Ulster Union Action Council in May 1977 failed to obtain the support that the 1974 strike had achieved – but the hostility between the two sections of the community remained strong. In 1979 the Shadow Secretary of State for Northern Ireland, Airey Neave, was assassinated while, later in the same year, Earl Mountbatten, uncle of the Queen, was murdered while on a fishing trip.

The policy of the Conservative government elected in 1979 (and re-elected in 1983) was that the future of Ulster was the responsibility of the inhabitants as a whole. However, it is clear that, as in the past, the sympathy of much of the Conservative Party – particularly among backbench MPs – lies with the Unionists. In 1981 a Northern Ireland Council, whose function would have been to advise the Secretary of State, was proposed but failed to gain the support of the political parties in Northern Ireland. The next year elections took place for a new Assembly consisting of seventy-eight seats but, following the election, a number of members refused to take their seats, while others withdrew – not surprisingly the contribution of the Assembly, which has a consultative role, was somewhat muted. In June 1986, the Assembly was dissolved by the British government, despite the protests of Unionist members. Developments in Northern Ireland are, of course, closely watched in Dublin and in 1983 the Irish government called a New Ireland Forum in the Republic to which the leading Northern Ireland political parties (with the exception of Sinn Fein which supports the Provisional IRA) were invited. However, the politicians of the North almost unanimously refused to participate in the Forum – the leaders of the Unionist parties saying that they would do everything in their power to frustrate its activities – while the British government refused to endorse the Irish initiative. However, intergovernmental discussions were being held and in November 1985 the Hillsborough Agreement was signed between Britain and the Irish Republic. This treaty for the first time gave Dublin an opportunity to be consulted on matters concerning Northern Ireland. Under the terms of the agreement an international conference was established, with an Irish minister sitting with the British Secretary of State. The agreement also provided for the setting up of a secretariat in Belfast staffed jointly by civil servants from Northern and Southern Ireland. Although Mrs Thatcher reiterated the pledge of successive British governments that there would be no change to the constitutional position of Northern Ireland, the Unionists promptly condemned the agreement. All the Unionist MPs sitting at Westminster resigned their seats and announced that they would stand for re-election on the issue of opposition to the agreement. At the subsequent by-elections held in January 1986, fourteen of the fifteen MPs who had resigned were re-elected but the fact that one of their number was defeated by a member of the SDLP tended to take the edge off their gesture. It was also rather galling for the Unionists that in most of the electoral contests the opposition parties declined to put up candidates, which meant that re-election was virtually certain. The Unionist MPs, however, claimed the result as a victory for the status quo and announced that they would continue to campaign against the attempts of the British and Irish governments to establish a dialogue. The Provisional IRA also let it be known that it, too, rejected the Hillsborough Agreement and that it would continue to campaign for a united Ireland.

Glossary

(The purpose of this glossary is to give the meaning of certain expressions and terms in the context in which they are used in the text. The meaning given here is not necessarily the only one.)

Abdication   Renunciation of rights to throne by sovereign. The most recent abdication was that of Edward VIII (the late Duke of Windsor) in 1936.

Act   Statute passed by both Houses of Parliament and given the Royal Assent.

Adjournment   Postponement of proceedings (for example, in Parliament) until another occasion.

Adoption meeting   Meeting at which a parliamentary candidate is chosen.

Anglican   Of the Church of England.

Appeal (legal)   To take a case to a higher court.

Audience (of royalty)   Interview with or presentation to the sovereign.

Back bencher   Member of Parliament who is not a member of the government (that is, not of ministerial rank) or the Shadow Cabinet.

Back-to-back houses   Houses with a common rear wall and no rear access (usually built in the late eighteenth or early nineteenth centuries).

Bail (legal)   Temporary release from custody on a security to appear for trial; also the security.

Ballot   Secret vote (introduced in British elections in 1872); *ballot paper* paper on which the vote is recorded; *ballot box* box in which the paper is inserted after the vote has been recorded.

Bank holiday   Public holiday in England and Wales, for example, Boxing Day (the day after Christmas), the Spring Bank Holiday.

Bar (legal)   Barristers collectively, or profession of barrister (barristers are 'called to the Bar' when they qualify).

Bench   Collective term for magistrates or judges when presiding in court.

Bill (political)   Draft of an Act of Parliament submitted to Parliament for debate.

Black Rod   Gentleman Usher of the Black Rod (so-called because he carries a black rod or stick), usher of the Lord Chamberlain's department of the royal household, also usher of the House of Lords.

Building society   Financial institution to which members lend money at a certain rate of interest and which in turn lends money for the purchase of property – usually houses.

By-election   Election in a single constituency during the life of Parliament following death or retirement of an MP.

Canvass   To try to obtain support for a candidate at an election by interviewing individual voters.

Census   Official counting of the population; in Great Britain a census has been taken every ten years since 1801.

Chief constable   Chief officer in police force outside London (in the Metropolitan Police District – roughly Greater London – and the City of London the chief officers are Commissioners of Police).

Circuit   District through which a judge travels when attending courts.

City (The)   City of London, particularly when referring to financial institutions such as Stock Exchange, banks, insurance companies, etc.

Civil List   Sum voted by Parliament for household and personal expenses of sovereign.

Civil servant   Salaried government official.

Civil War   War (1642–6) between Parliament and King Charles I. The king was defeated and was executed in 1649.

Classifieds   Small advertisements appearing in columns of newspapers or journals classified under headings such as 'For Sale', 'Situations Vacant' (jobs), etc.

Coalition   Combination of two or more political parties to form a Government (or Opposition).

Constituency   Body of voters – in parliamentary terms, area for which an MP is elected and which he represents in Parliament.

Council house   House built and maintained by a local authority (that is, a council) and rented to tenants.

'Daily' (paper)   Newspaper that appears six days a week (cf. 'Sunday').

Diocese   Area under the authority of a bishop.

Disestablish (ecclesiastical)   To withdraw state support and patronage from Church.

Display advertisement   Advertisement that is spread over a portion of a page of a newspaper or journal (cf. 'Classifieds').

Dissolution (of Parliament)   Bringing a session of Parliament to an end.

Division   Separation of Parliament into two for counting votes.

Ecclesiastical   Relating to the Church or to clergymen.

Electorate (parliamentary)   People over 18 years of age who are entitled to vote in a parliamentary election.

Equity (legal)   System of law existing alongside statute law and common law which supersedes them when they conflict.

Filibuster   To prolong debate on a Bill so that its passage through Parliament cannot be completed in the time available. (An American term.)

Flat racing (the flat)   Horses racing over level ground without hedges or ditches.

Fleet Street   Street in London where there are a large number of national (and provincial) newspaper offices.

Friendly Society   Association whose members pay contributions to insure financial help in sickness or old age.

Front bencher   Member of the Government or senior member of Opposition (usually in Cabinet or Shadow Cabinet).

Graduate   Person who holds a university degree.

Honour   Title or award granted by the sovereign (almost always on ministerial advice). Honours are traditionally awarded twice a year, at New Year, and on the sovereign's official birthday. They can be given on other occasions, for example, 'Dissolution of Parliament' (see above).

Immigrant   Usually in context 'Commonwealth immigrant' referring to person originally coming from 'new' Commonwealth: West Indies, Pakistan (which is no longer a Commonwealth member), India, Bangladesh, etc.

Incumbent (ecclesiastical)   Clergyman holding a living (as priest).

Independent (political)   Politician who belongs to no political party or group.

Jacobite   Supporter of the Stuart line and of the descendants of James II who abdicated in 1688.

Junior (legal)   Barrister who assists senior counsel (barrister) in presentation of a case in court.

Kirk   The Church of Scotland as distinct from the Church of England (kirk: Scottish form of 'church').

Living (ecclesiastical)   Benefice, that is, in Church of England, income-producing property supporting a priest.

Lobby (political)   In sense of division lobbies, two chambers into which MPs go when they vote, one for 'Ayes' and one for 'Noes'. Also place where MPs meet constituents, journalists, etc. (hence 'lobby correspondents', journalists particularly concerned with politics).

Lord Chamberlain   A prominent official of the Royal Household.

Lord Protector   Title held by Oliver Cromwell as head of state 1653–8, and briefly by his son Richard.

Maisonette   Small house, or completely self-contained part of large house used as dwelling.

Marginal seat (political)   Constituency where the majority of the sitting member is low, which means the seat might be won by a rival party at an election (cf. 'Safe seat').

Middle Ages   Historical period from (roughly) AD 1,000 to *c.* 1450.

Minister (political)   Person controlling or administering department of state. The most powerful minister is the Prime Minister, also known as the First Lord of the Treasury. Other key ministers are the Chancellor of the Exchequer (finance minister), Home Secretary (Secretary of State for Home Affairs), Foreign Secretary and Lod Chancellor. Large 'departments' are headed by secretaries of state, e.g. Secretary of State for Defence, Secretary of State for Health and Social Security. In the departments there may be junior ministers, e.g. Minister for Transport Industries within the Department of the Environment, and ministers of state. Junior ministers are known either as parliamentary secretaries or parliamentary under-secretaries of state, depending on the status of the minister in charge of the department.

Ministry (political)   A government department, for example, Department of the Environment, Ministry of Defence. Administered by a politician (see 'Minister') and staffed by civil servants.

Mortgage   Money loan advanced by building society, council, etc. for purchase of dwelling or other property, with the house, etc. being used as security.

Nationalisation   Taking over of business concerns by the state.

Nonconformist   Person who does not accept the doctrines of an established Church, especially the Church of England, usually excluding Roman Catholics.

Open University   Institution (first students accepted 1971) which provides university-level courses in students' homes by means of television and radio lectures and correspondence courses.

Oxbridge   Oxford and Cambridge Universities, that is, the ancient universities.

Point-to-point   Cross-country race for horses.

Polytechnic   Institution of higher education financed and controlled by local authorities.

Postgraduate   Student studying for a higher degree, (for example, MA, Master of Arts, PhD, Doctor of Philosophy) or diploma.

Precedent (legal)   Previous decision or action which provides an authoritative rule for similar cases.

Presbyterian Church   Church governed by a council or assembly of 'elders' or officials, especially the Church of Scotland.

Provinces   England outside London (hence 'provincial').

Puisne judge (legal)   Judge in a superior court of rank lower than chief justice.

Question Time   Period during parliamentary day set aside for MPs to question ministers.

Rates   Local property tax.
Referendum   Direct vote by citizens on a political issue.
Returning officer   Official responsible for arranging and conducting an election

Safe seat (political)   Constituency where the sitting member has a large majority and there is little or no danger of any rival political party winning the seat at an election (cf. 'Marginal seat').
Sandwich course   Course (especially at polytechnics and technical colleges) where students spend alternate periods of time at work and studying at the institution.
Semi-detached house   House that has one common wall with another house.
Session (political)   Period for which Parliament sits.
Shadow Cabinet   Group composed of the leader of the Opposition and his or her senior colleagues in Parliament.
Sheriff   Official representing the Crown in counties with various ceremonial, judicial and electoral functions.
'Stand for Parliament'   Attempt to get elected to Parliament by being nominated at an election (the American expression is 'run for office').
Steeplechasing   Horse racing over hedges and ditches.
Suffrage (political)   The right to vote.
'Sunday'   Newspaper published on Sundays.
Synod   Assembly of clergy (and lay representatives) for discussing and deciding ecclesiastical affairs.

The Tower (of London)   Fortress and royal palace traditionally used as place of imprisonment and execution for offenders against the state – now a museum, though still garrisoned.
Tudor period   The Tudors came to power in 1485 when Henry Tudor (later Henry VII) defeated Richard III. The fifth and last Tudor monarch, Elizabeth I, died in 1603.

Undergraduate   Student studying for first degree.
Underwriter   Person who carries on an insurance business.

Verdict (legal)   Decision of jury as to whether the accused in a trial is guilty or not guilty.

Westminster   Parliament.

Whitehall Area of London where the most important ministries are found, for example, the Treasury, Home Office, Foreign Office.

Whip (political) (a) Party official responsible for maintaining party discipline; (b); Letter setting out instructions for attendances at debates sent to MPs by the Whips' office.

Workhouse Institution, especially in nineteenth-century Britain, where those unable to support themselves were given food, shelter and work, all of a low standard (see novels of Dickens and Hardy, for example).

Writ Written command from sovereign, court, etc. requiring some specific action, for example, writ for an election.

Select Bibliography

General

Central Office of Information, *Britain: An Official Handbook* (HMSO, annual).

Central Statistical Office, *Annual Abstract of Statistics* (HMSO, annual).

Central Statistical Office, *Social Trends* (HMSO, annual).

Jowell, R., and Airey, C., *British Social Attitudes 1984* (Gower, 1984).

Jowell, R., and Witherspoon, S., *British Social Attitudes 1985* (Gower, 1985).

Jowell, R., Witherspoon, S., and Brook, L., *British Social Attitudes 1986* (Gower, 1986).

Sampson, A., *Anatomy of Britain* (Hodder, 1962).

Sampson, A., *A New Anatomy of Britain* (Hodder, 1971).

Sampson, A., *The Changing Anatomy of Britain* (Hodder, 1982; paperback, Coronet, 1983).

Whitaker's Almanac (J. Whitaker & Sons, annual).

Historical and Geographical Background

Blake, R., *The Decline of Power 1915–1964* (Granada, 1985).

Fleure, H. J., *A Natural History of Man in Britain* (Collins/Fontana, 1971).

Hill, C. P., *British Economic and Social History 1700–1982*, 5th edn (Edward Arnold, 1985).

Hoskins, W. G., *The Making of the English Landscape*, 3rd edn (Hodder, 1977).

Marwick, A., *Britain in Our Century* (Thames & Hudson, 1984).

Sked, A., and Cook, C., *Post-War Britain: A Political History* (Penguin, 1984).

Stamp, L. Dudley, and Beaver, S. H., *The British Isles: A Geographic and Economic Survey* (Longman, 1971).

Taylor, A. J. P., *England 1914–1945* (Oxford University Press, 1965 and 1975; paperback, Penguin, 1970).

Thomson, D., *England in the Twentieth Century*, 2nd edn edited by Geoffrey Warner (Penguin, 1981).

Trueman, A. E., *Geology and Scenery in England and Wales* (Penguin, 1971).

Government and Politics

Birch, A. H., *The British System of Government*, 5th edn (Allen & Unwin, 1982).

Blake, R., *The Conservative Party from Peel to Churchill* (Eyre & Spottiswoode, 1970).

Blondel, J., *Voters, Parties and Leaders* (Penguin, 1969).

Butler, D., and Kavanagh, D., *The British General Election of 1983* (Macmillan, 1984).

Butler, D., and Butler, G., *British Political Facts 1900–1985*, 6th edn (Macmillan, 1986).

Hanson, A. H., and Walles, M., *Governing Britain*, 4th edn (Fontana, 1984).

McKenzie, R. T., *British Political Parties* (Heinemann, 1964).

Pelling, H., *A Short History of the Labour Party* (Macmillan, 1972).

Punnett, R. M., *British Government and Politics*, 5th edn (Gower, 1987).

Richards, P. G., *Mackintosh's The Government and Politics of Britain*, 6th edn (Hutchinson, 1984).

Local Government

Byrne, T., *Local Government in Britain*, 2nd edn (Penguin, 1983).

Keith-Lucas, B., and Richards, P. G., *A History of Local Government in the Twentieth Century* (Allen & Unwin, 1978).

The Monarchy

Duncan, A., *The Reality of Monarchy* (Heinemann, 1970; paperback, Pan, 1973).

Hamilton, W., *My Queen and I* (Quartet, 1975).

Lacey, R., *Majesty: Elizabeth II and the House of Windsor* (Hutchinson, 1977).

Martin, K., *The Crown and the Establishment* (Hutchinson, 1962; paperback, Penguin, 1963).

The Legal System

Berlins, M., and Dyer, C., *The Law Machine* (Penguin, 1982).

Roshier, B., and Teff, H., *Law and Society in England* (Tavistock, 1980).

The Welfare State

Bennett, F., *Your Social Security*, 2nd edn (Penguin, 1984).
Brown, M., *Introduction to Social Administration in Britain*, 6th edn (Hutchinson, 1985).
Lynes, T., *The Penguin Guide to Supplementary Benefits*, 5th edn (Penguin, 1985).
Titmuss, R., *Essays on the Welfare State* (Allen & Unwin, 1963).
Ward, S., *Social Security at Work* (Pluto, 1982).

Education

Hewton, E., *Education in Recession* (Allen & Unwin, 1986).
Lawson, J. and Silver, H., *A Social History of Education in England* (Methuen, 1973).

Industry and Commerce

Boddy, M., *The Building Societies* (Macmillan, 1980).
Cairncross, F., and Keeley, P., *The Guardian Guide to the Economy* (Methuen, 1981).
Clarke, W., *Inside the City* (Allen & Unwin, 1983).
Douglas Hamilton, J., *Stockbroking Tomorrow* (Macmillan, 1986).
Hall, S. G., and Atkinson, F., *Oil and the British Economy* (Croom Helm, 1983).
McCarthy, W. E. J., *Trade Unions*, 2nd edn (Penguin, 1985).
McRae, H. and Cairncross, F., *Capital City*, 2nd edn (Methuen, 1984).
More, M., *The Politics of Banking* (Macmillan, 1984).
Morris, D., *The Economic System in the UK*, 3rd edn (Oxford University Press, 1985).
National Economic Development Council, *British Industrial Performance* (NEDC), 1985).
Pringle, R., *Banking in Britain* (Methuen, 1975).
Revell, J., *The British Financial System* (Macmillan, 1973).
Williams, K., Williams, J., and Thomas, D., *Why Are the British Bad at Manufacturing?* (Routledge & Kegan Paul, 1983).

Life in Britain

Bellini, J., *Rule Britannia* (Cape, 1981).
Booker, C., *The Neophiliacs* (Collins, 1969; paperback, Fontana, 1970).

Select Bibliography

Centre for Contemporary Cultural Studies, *The Empire Strikes Back: Race and Racism in 70s Britain* (Hutchinson, 1982).

Fletcher, R., *The Family and Marriage in Britain* (Penguin, 1969).

Hoggart, R., *The Uses of Literacy* (Chatto & Windus, 1957; paperback, Penguin, 1969).

Nairn, T., *The Break-Up of Britain* (Verso, 1981).

Office of Population Censuses and Surveys, *The General Household Survey* (HMSO, 1985, annual).

Reid, I., *Social Class Differences in Britain*, 2nd edn (Grant McIntyre, 1980).

Ryder, J., and Silver, H., *Modern English Society 1850–1970* (Methuen, 1970).

Townsend, P., *Poverty in the United Kingdom* (Allen Lane/Penguin, 1979).

Young, M., and Willmott, P., *Family and Kinship in East London* (Routledge & Kegan Paul, 1973).

Young, M., and Willmott, P., *The Symmetrical Family* (Routledge & Kegan Paul, 1973).

Press and Broadcasting

Briggs, A., *The History of Broadcasting in the United Kingdom*: Vol. I The Birth of Broadcasting, 1961; Vol. II The Golden Age of Wireless, 1965; Vol. III The War of Words, 1970; all published by Oxford University Press.

Dunkley, C., *Television Today and Tomorrow* (Penguin, 1985).

Index